Your Finest Hour Is Now

Lessons in Leadership

A leader's guide to improve yourself, inspire others,

and achieve better results

By STEVE MATTIOLI

Published by PWTPublishing

A Division of The Hive Consulting Group Inc.

Greater Toronto Area, ON Canada

publisher@pwt.global

First paperback edition November 30, 2023

Book design by PWTPublishing

Paperback ISBN: 978-1-7388840-8-7

Digital Book ISBN: 978-1-7388840-9-4

www.MattioliSolutions.com

Steve.mattioli@icloud.com

Limits of Liability and Disclaimer of Warranty

The author and publisher shall not be liable for the reader's misuse of this material. This book is for strictly informational and educational purposes.

Disclaimer

The views expressed are those of the author and do not reflect the official policy or position of the publisher or Powerful Women Today.

Copyright Use and Public Information

Unless otherwise noted, images have been used according to public information laws.

CONTENTS

Preface

I began writing this book over five years ago. My goal is to pass along the lessons I learned during my career that will help you become a better leader. I've always had the ability to take complex topics and make them easy to understand. For example, one of my roles in my previous job was taking federal regulations and making them easier for the public to comprehend and comply with. I use that same skill in this book to tackle the topics that help leaders succeed.

I've been in a leadership role for most of my adult life, encompassing over thirty years. During that time, I acquired knowledge and skills that helped me succeed as a leader. I've been consistently promoted and earned awards for my leadership ability. I've seen what it takes to get promoted and grow as a leader. Unfortunately, I've also seen what can hinder leaders and hold them back from their full potential. I'm now ready to share that knowledge with you.

I wrote this book about leadership to be helpful, fun to read, and easy to understand. This book will show you the principles and techniques that lead to successful outcomes. You will learn how to improve yourself, build employee loyalty, avoid common pitfalls, navigate tricky situations, and apply time-tested wisdom for better results. My goal in writing this book was to help you become a better, more impactful leader. You will be better prepared to lead after reading this book because each topic I cover comes from hands-on experience, with actual employees, in real situations.

Before we begin, let me tell you a little about my background. I served thirty-five years with the Federal Motor Carrier Safety Administration (FMCSA), an agency of the U.S. Department of Transportation. I spent most of that time as a supervisor and leader, holding critical positions for most of my career. I served in several locations with the organization, including North Carolina, Ohio, Illinois, and California. My last assignment was as the supervisor in charge of the California division, the 2nd largest in the agency.

Before joining the federal government, I was employed in the trucking industry and served four years in the United States Marine Corps Reserves. I earned a bachelor's degree from the University of Akron and was a licensed private pilot. I live in Folsom, California, with my wife, Dottie, and pet dog, Ace.

Please stay in touch with me by email at: steve.mattioli@icloud.com, and visit my website at MattioliSolutions.com for more leadership articles, training videos, and other helpful tools for leaders.

In this book, references to the time I worked for the FMCSA will be abbreviated as "government" or "my agency."

Name changes

While the names of individuals I worked with, for privacy, were changed, the dialogue and events occurred as described.

Introduction

———

I'll never forget that morning in January 1992. I was so excited to go to work. It was one of those days when you can't wait to get up and get started. This was a big day for me; I had been promoted to my first supervisory position after four and a half years of hard work, and I was beginning my new job in a brand-new city. As I drove to my new office in the early morning hours, I saw the tall, glittering buildings of downtown Columbus, Ohio, come into view. *Wow,* I thought to myself, *this is it. I've finally arrived.* I couldn't contain my excitement. This was my first promotion, the first step on my ladder of success. I took it all in as I drove downtown—the city, the lights, the morning so full of possibilities—and before I knew it, I was standing in front of the office entrance, taking a deep breath and opening the door to a new chapter in my career.

I was greeted by a friendly receptionist who gave me a whirlwind tour of the office and led me down a narrow office hallway, where she introduced me to my new boss. He was a tough-looking, tall, older man with neatly combed-back grey hair who had spent twenty years as a state trooper with the Ohio State Highway Patrol. In the 1960s, it was said that he led a group of officers that went into a prison during a riot to take back control of the facility. Yeah, this guy was as tough as they come. He welcomed me in and introduced me to the other employees, lots of new names and faces that I frantically tried to remember through my first-day nerves. I could tell everyone was sizing me up, trying to determine whether I would be great or awful to work with from the quick handshakes and polite greetings. I couldn't blame them. We both knew how much control I would have over their professional lives in the future. Everything was about to change, yet nobody knew what to expect from me.

As I settled into my new office, the gravity of the situation finally hit me. Yes, I had done the jobs of those I was about to supervise. And yes, I had proven myself to be capable in their field. I deserved this promotion over all of the others who applied for it. I had the knowledge, skills, and motivation to do the job well. *I'm ready for this*, I told myself. *At least I think I am.* In the Navy, sailors call the ship's wheel the conn, and that morning, I felt like I was taking control of the conn of a vast ship, the success—or failure—of which I would now be held accountable. This was the promotion I had been waiting for, and it was time to show everyone what I was capable of. I was excited—and scared.

In the few quiet moments of that first day on the job, the weight of my new responsibilities hit me—hard. I began to think of all of the critical decisions I now had to make. *Will I embarrass myself or the agency? Am I ready for this? Will the employees accept me? Do I even know how to lead them? What if I mess up?*

If you're anything like me, those same fears and doubts have gone through your mind when taking on a new and vital leadership role. These are common feelings. Everyone has high expectations of you, and your every move is carefully watched and frequently scrutinized. Over the years, I've learned that feelings of both courage and fear come with promotions. Courage is looking at your past and knowing that you can do whatever you set your mind to. Looking back at your past accomplishments gives you the confidence to accomplish bigger and better things. This is confidence in yourself and your abilities. But fear? Fear of failure? That's not supposed to be there.

Failure was on my mind on that first day of my promotion. Up until this point in my career, I had been responsible for one and only one person—me. Now I would be responsible for many. Whereas before, I only had to make sure my work was exemplary, now I had to make sure everyone's work was good. Whereas before, I only had to achieve my own goals, now I would be responsible for the goals of an entire office. *At least my boss will train me on what to do,* I told myself. Wrong. "I'm so sick of running these employees," he said as he showed me piles of meticulously kept, handwritten records and lists of every aspect of the program and the employees. I tried to hide my shock. *No computer? What is this, the Middle Ages?* "Make it work, Steve," he told me.

And with that, my leadership career in the United States Federal Government began.[1] Over the next three decades, I would be leading in more prominent and challenging roles with the Federal Motor Carrier Safety Administration (FMCSA). I would become the leader—the division administrator—of the FMCSA's Ohio Division office and be promoted to lead two other Division Offices in Illinois and California. I've received some of the highest recognitions from my agency, including being named a co-chair of a national workgroup that revised the agency's entire enforcement process. And it all started in that little office in Columbus, Ohio.

Before my time in the U.S. Government, I served in the U.S. Marine Corps Reserves. I joined the U.S. Marine Corps when I was eighteen years old and spent four years in a reserve infantry unit. Starting as a rifleman, I worked my way up to become a fire team leader, a platoon radio operator, and a rifle squad leader, eventually achieving the rank of Corporal. When I graduated from Marine Corps boot camp at Parris Island, South Carolina, one of the commanding officers gave my platoon somewhat of a commencement address. He told us that someday the success or failure of a mission might come down to just one Marine. One. And the Marine Corps had trained us with the knowledge, skills, and stamina to be that one Marine. All of our training, all the suffering we endured, and the long

[1]   Federal Highway Administration and Federal Motor Carrier Safety Administration.

days full of physical exertion were to ensure that each of us would succeed if we were that one Marine. And you may be that one person with whom success or failure—of your company, your office, your team, or your business—rests. My goal is to provide you with the information you need to succeed.

My thirty-plus years of leadership have taught me how to engage with employees, communicate effectively, and accomplish personal and professional goals. I've learned how to lead diverse groups of people and, in turn, how to be led by them. I've learned how to earn the respect of others and how important it is to show others respect in return. I've learned how to be tough and how to be kind, how to win, how to discipline and praise, how to be patient, and how to manage priorities. I've also had my fair share of failures and stumbles along the way. Leadership is a skill that must be continually worked on because one never arrives at perfection. It's a continuous learning process.

Leadership is vitally important to the success of any organization. A leader makes the difference between success and failure. A leader mobilizes others to produce much greater results than the sum of their parts. A leader changes things for the better. One good leader is all it takes to change the course of history. A leader overcomes where others fail. When others are pessimistic, a leader is confident; when others are downcast, a leader encourages. When others can't see a way forward, a leader finds a path. A leader cares for the people they lead. A country, an army, a company, or a small business all need strong, effective leaders. Wherever you may work, you need to be that leader. And this book will help you be that leader.

When people think of leaders today, they think of presidents of the United States, such as Abraham Lincoln, or the CEOs of incredibly successful companies, like Steve Jobs of Apple, Jeff Bezos of Amazon, or Elon Musk of Tesla. These are great leaders in their respective fields, and there is much that we can learn from them. But these examples are just one aspect of leadership. There are thousands of employees working behind the scenes to ensure that day-to-day operations run smoothly within these companies and organizations. From policy advisors, software engineers, and floor supervisors to content editors and human resource officers, these leaders would not be successful without the thousands of other leaders working on the front lines leading employees every day and achieving results.

It takes more than a CEO to run a company. Regardless of what their title may be, every leader is crucial to a company's bottom line. In my leadership career, I've learned that the employees in the lower leadership positions are the most critical to an organization's success. Not only do these employees control tremendous amounts of resources, but their efforts motivate and guide those who directly impact clients and customers. These are the unsung heroes. Without them, big companies couldn't thrive. You may not be leading a country through tumultuous times, leading an army in battle, or serving as the CEO of a large corporation, but your success as a leader is just as critical whether you realize it or not. The time and effort you invest into your supervisory skills greatly impact your organization; in fact, its success or failure can hinge on your ability to lead.

Leadership isn't complicated, but it certainly isn't easy. It may be easy to boss people around, but it takes skill to lead others successfully. It's only by leading others that one can accomplish great results. Cultivating a successful team can release exponential results that wouldn't be possible by yourself. If you are currently in a leadership position or plan to be, this book is your guide to becoming a successful and effective leader. No matter your background, you too can have a successful career leading others. Throughout this book, I'll show you the principles and skills you need to be a well-respected and impactful leader. It doesn't matter what career stage you're in, which industry you work in, or what kind of job you have:

> If you lead others in any capacity, whether you're a first-time supervisor or a seasoned leader, this book is for you. I'll show you how to avoid common mistakes and keep improving in your pursuit of becoming a better leader.

If you're a small business owner, this book is for you. I'll teach you how to lead your employees effectively so you can spend more time focused on running your business.

If you're stressed out and having a tough time leading others, this book is for you. I'll explain how you can reduce your stress levels and positively deal with people.

If you're not yet in a leadership position but you want to be, this book is definitely for you. It will give you a huge advantage as you progress toward becoming a leader and will prepare you to take the lead when an opportunity presents itself.

You have what it takes to be a great leader, one who inspires confidence in others and achieves whatever you set your mind to. Are you ready to lead? Are you ready to move forward? Buckle up, and let's get started. We're going to start with something really simple—and you've known it all along. Before We Begin...

Chapter 1

TAKE A SELFIE

Lessons in Self-Awareness

What do you see when you take a selfie? Obviously, you see yourself, but what else do you see? What else *should* you see? I've always been amused that the person I see in the mirror does not look exactly like the one I see when I take a selfie on my phone. Somehow it's a bit different. I'm more critical of a selfie than the person I see in the mirror because I notice more things about myself. I can take pictures from different angles to see myself in ways I usually can't. I can zoom in and get real close to see the flaws in my skin or how thin my hair really is, or how genuine my smile looks. I can change the lighting or the background through my phone's seemingly endless photo settings.

A selfie exposes me somewhat differently than a mirror does. It helps me spot visual flaws that I don't usually notice. It allows me to see myself precisely as others see me, and sometimes I don't like what it shows. Sometimes I can't believe I look like that! Thank goodness for the delete button.

Leadership is a lot like taking a selfie. I know that might sound crazy, but let me explain. You have your personal mirror, which makes you look pretty good. But under different angles, different lighting, and different situations, you may not look as good as you think you do. You may not be as good as you think. This is how the world really sees you. Everybody can see your flaws—even if you can't. Others see you from a multitude of angles, some that you are blind to.

And just like an actual selfie, some flaws are fixable, and some aren't. I can't fix the fact that I hardly have any hair on my head despite what the magic potions sold on TV promise. But once I know this and accept it as a fact, I can still look great as I deal with reality. I dress profession-ally and keep a tight shave on my hair so I look my best, and I have a positive attitude that exudes confidence. I compensate for the issues I see in my selfie, even if I can't change them.

> *"You have your personal mirror, which makes you look pretty good. But under different angles, different lighting, and different situations, you may not look as good as you think you do. You may not be as good as you think"*

To be a great leader, you need to take a selfie—an *ac-curate* self-assessment. I want to emphasize the word ac-curate. You will only be able to improve as a leader when you look at yourself with complete honesty. We fool our-selves all the time into believing things about us that aren't true. It's that posed look you see in the mirror versus an unflattering selfie angle. Unless we deal with an accurate assessment of our strengths and weaknesses, we'll never become great leaders.

It's crucial that you know your flaws and strengths and which habits or attitudes you always default to. Imagine that you need to cross a river, and you're examining a boat that could help you get to the other side. You need to make sure the boat has no holes, especially below the waterline, where water could pour in. As you examine the boat, you find a small hole. What do you do at this point? Do you toss the boat aside and try to find a new one? Maybe, if you had the time and money for a new one, but this is your only option. So you say to yourself, *You know what? I'll just patch the hole and keep an eye on it so it doesn't leak.* The small hole in the boat doesn't make the entire boat useless. It can be repaired so the boat can function properly. And if the first patch doesn't work, there are always other types of patches out there that will get the job done. But if you ignore this flaw and attempt to cross the river, the boat and your life could be in serious jeopardy.

Here's a simple fact about all leaders—they all have holes in their boats. Nobody is a perfect leader, and nobody has all of the right talents to lead. If you could imagine leaders as boats, they would all have a bunch of patched-up holes in them, and some of them would be patched up multiple times. The idea of a perfect leader is a myth. Every leader has flaws that make them imperfect at what they do. You have them, and so do I. Steve Jobs of Apple had them, and so did Bill Gates of Microsoft and Jeff Bezos of Amazon. Steve Jobs was known as one of the brightest creative geniuses of his time, yet he struggled with his anger, arrogance, and relationships with employees. It cost him dearly. He nearly lost his career and his company because of it. Every great leader has a similar story to tell. Yet each one has learned how to overcome their flaws to become the best leaders they can be.

Some flaws are internal; they are a part of who we are. One of my biggest internal flaws is that I am reserved. You don't have to ask me to be quiet; I already am. It's my nature, my default setting. When I'm in a room with a lot of people, I don't talk much. And I usually don't speak up in group settings. I prefer to observe everything and listen to everyone in the background. Being reserved is not a sin, and it's certainly not a crime. Some even say it's a good trait to have. As they say, you are who you are. Since I've been this way since birth, why fix it? Well, eventually, I found out that being reserved is not always compatible with outstanding leadership. I still received promotions from my superiors since I worked hard and was good at what I did. But the more I stayed in my comfort zone of being quiet, the more it became a blind spot for me. It held me back from bigger opportunities.

Then along came my new boss, D. D made things happen. He was outgoing, smart, well-liked, and had the ear of top leadership. He always found a way to lead his employees through difficult situations. One sign of a great leader is that they help others become great leaders. D noticed how my silence held me back from opportunities that would advance my career. He knew that I couldn't become a better leader without addressing the blind spot my naturally quiet demeanor had become. D and I were at a meeting together when he pulled me aside and said he wanted to speak with me. What he told me changed the trajectory of my career. "Steve, you need to speak up in these meetings. People respect you, and they need to hear what you have to say." The second he said those words, I knew he was exactly right. I had to overcome my shyness and speak.

And I did. I was later appointed as a co-chair of a national working group to re-engineer the agency's enforcement program. The team I led developed a better performance-based process that completely changed how the agency assessed risk and assigned resources. That system is still in use today. I was placed on a team that helped institute an electronic document management system for the agency. That system is still in use today, too. I received promotions to the division administrator positions in Illinois and later in California. I received recognition for my efforts at national award ceremonies from my agency and the Department of Transportation. I received dozens of superior ratings that highlighted my accomplishments and rewarded me financially. I became a great public presenter and gave many presentations to the trucking industry, the public, state officials, leadership, and colleagues in my agency. In summary, I overcame my internal flaw and succeeded beyond my dreams. Overcoming opened up a world of possibilities for me.

> *"In summary, I overcame my internal flaw and succeeded beyond my dreams. Overcoming opened up a world of possibilities for me. "*

Now wait a minute, you might be saying. A few paragraphs ago, you said you were still quiet! I am. But I have learned how to put this aside when I'm at work. And it wasn't as difficult as I thought it would be. All I had to do was be willing to change, and I did. I am still reserved and always will be, but I have learned how to manage it in professional settings to be the best leader I can be. Just like the hole in the boat that needs to be patched before it can successfully cross a river, I've fixed this, and I keep an eye on it. I adjust when I see that I may be leaning back into my quiet nature too much.

To be a great leader, you need to know your internal flaws. Challenge yourself to be brutally honest. What are your innate personality traits, and how do these traits interact with others? What is your default setting? Are you a people person or quiet like me? These are essential questions to ask yourself as you begin your leadership journey. Your style—the real you—is the starting point, but you may need to work on some aspects here and there and overcome your weaknesses to become the leader you want to be.

While some flaws—like my reservedness are internal, others are external. Maybe you are not the best writer or presenter. Perhaps you don't have the analytical skills you need to track progress on your goals or to tackle a big project at work. These flaws are not who you are, but they are nonetheless holes in your boat that can prevent you from reaching your full potential. Often all you need to overcome these external flaws is more education, technical skills, or training in a particular subject. For many years I devoted time each week to read up on various topics to help me in my job. If I felt like I was falling behind in communicating effectively or managing my priorities, I would consult books, online articles, and reference materials to sharpen my sword. When I needed more technical knowledge about self-driving vehicles and their potential effect on my work with the trucking industry, I studied and learned about the Global Positioning System and how it worked. I did these things because I identified deficiencies in my job knowledge that I knew I had to address to succeed.

You have a leadership flaw that's hindering you from achieving your best results. It could be that you are too loud and don't listen to others enough. It might be arrogance, impatience, or lack of communication skills. Whatever your flaw is, you must first spend time identifying it and then take steps to correct it. If you need stronger writing skills, read up on the elements of business writing. If you lack effective public-speaking skills, practice more or take a class. If your flaw is part of your personality, learn how to make it work for you and not against you. If you are generally loud and outgoing, practice being quiet and listening to others more. If you usually are quiet and shy like I am, practice being more talkative and outgoing. Overcoming your weaknesses is a critical piece of the foundation you need to lead effectively. Don't blow by this quickly. Take your time and commit to the process.

I've heard people say countless times, "Well, this is just who I am, and I can't change." What they are really saying is that they don't want to change. Throughout my career, I've noticed that those who don't address their obvious flaws eventually hit a brick wall. It reduces their ability to progress further in their career. They die on the vine. And then that flaw presents itself during a big presentation or in front of senior staff, and they are permanently scarred by it.

If you want to be an effective leader and reach your full potential, you have no choice—you must fix the holes in your boat. Addressing your flaws—internal or external—is more a matter of will than ability. You have what it takes to overcome your flaws. All you have to do now is "take a selfie," an accurate self-assessment of yourself that will help you locate and address the shortcomings that others around you already see.

Many products on the market will help you do this. Tools such as 360-degree feedback assessments can provide you with valuable input from your peers, co-workers, and managers. Other tools, such as the Myers-Briggs Personality Test, assess your personality type and help you understand more about who you are and how you approach decisions. Similarly, the University of Southern California's Leadership Style Self-Assessment tool helps you understand your leadership style and how it impacts your performance in the office. The Institute for Health and Human Potential provides an Emotional Intelligence Assessment that helps you determine how your ability to perceive emotions affects your ability to manage others in the workplace. These are just a tiny sample of the wide variety of tools available to you as a leader.

Years ago, a friend named Frank took a 360-degree feedback survey with his employees and was shocked by the results. He discovered that some of them didn't think he was an effective communicator. He had supervised these employees for quite some time and thought he had a great working relationship with all of them. Weeks later, he was still stunned and upset that his employees had somehow betrayed him. He didn't see the flaws in his communication skills, but everyone else around him did. The survey results were an eye-opener for him and helped him address a weakness he never knew he had.

You may be upset with the results of your self-assessment. It hurts when others point out a flaw you didn't think you had. It's easy to react with anger and shock as my friend did, but remember that your peers, coworkers, and supervisors are only trying to help you. The holes they point out to you will sink your boat if you don't fix them. Someday you will thank them for helping you keep your boat afloat. Thank goodness for those around us who are honest enough to share feedback in a positive way! While it may hurt at first, this is a necessary step in the process, and you will see the value of it as long as you keep a positive attitude.

If these assessment tools do not fit your situation or finances, then good old-fashioned talking with friends, colleagues, and others who know you well is the best option. As good and helpful as these assessment tools can be, my best insights came from people I worked with, like my old boss, D. My coworkers knew my flaws and were kind enough to share them with me in positive, uplifting ways. I always prefer this improvement method and have personally grown more from it than any other assessment tool. Like D, I provide my feedback to other leaders so they can learn and advance in their professional development.

"If these assessment tools do not fit your situation or finances, then good old-fashioned talking with friends, colleagues, and others who know you well is the best option."

Don't be afraid to confront your internal and external flaws head-on. It's the only way you will become a better leader and help those around you achieve great results. Critically assess the information others provide you with an open mind that is always looking for ways to improve. Above all else, make a habit of evaluating your skills routinely. This isn't something you can do once and be done with. You may have fixed the holes in your boat years ago, but more may have developed in your blind spot. Keep on the lookout for them, keep fixing them, and keep taking your selfies.

Chapter 1
Lessons in Self-Awareness
Key takeaway and applied knowledge

Take it Further: Discuss the chapter with a friend or colleague and get their perspective on your selfie. Identify one area that you can improve upon and then take a step to address it.

Chapter 2

"SANTA CLAUS IS DEAD." WHAT?

Lessons in Reality

Santa Claus is dead. That's from a financial book I read many years ago.[1] Well, I thought to myself, that's not very positive. I mean, I suspected that Santa isn't real, but did the book have to say it? Right before it told me Santa was dead, it said to give up on any hope of getting rich quickly. I was getting a negative vibe from just the first few pages of this book. *Doesn't everyone want to be rich? I thought. Isn't a financial book supposed to be full of uplifting stories about people getting rich and making easy money? OK, Santa is dead, and I can't get rich quickly. Nothing more to read in this book, I thought.*

But despite the negative vibe, something in me urged me to keep reading. The book also said I could get rich slowly, and I'd be foolish not to try. That sounded a little better to me. I read on. The book stated that I could become rich if I saved money over long periods and invested it wisely. The author would show me how all of this worked. I was hooked! I bought the book. Over

---

1   Robert R. Gardiner, The Dean Witter Guide to Personal Investing, 1989, p.11

thirty years have passed since I first read that book, and to this day, it remains one of my favorite financial books.

The best part about the book is that it is honest and genuine on the first page. Free stuff and easy success, like Santa Claus, are not real. Many financial books promise overnight wealth and easy success where everyone becomes a millionaire. But these are a mirage. If you want to be financially successful, you have to plan, invest wisely, and give it time to accumulate. Trying to get rich quickly will only lead you to make all kinds of bad decisions. But if you do it the right way, you can achieve your financial goals.

> *"Free stuff and easy success, like Santa Claus, are not real. Many financial books promise overnight wealth and easy success where everyone becomes a millionaire. But these are a mirage."*

The same is true with becoming a great leader. Leadership is challenging, and it requires hard work and patience to see lasting results. Being honest and authentic with yourself about this process and the challenges it brings is essential whether you are preparing to become a leader for the first time or are seeking to elevate your skills. You must be willing to take on the stress and the long hours that come with the position. You have to be ready to handle the plethora of problems that come your way. It's hard work, both mentally and physically. The principles we'll cover in this book take time, patience, and consistency; success won't happen overnight. There are no shortcuts to becoming a great leader. Real leadership is not different from most good things in life that require dedication, time, and hard work.

I like it when someone tells me the truth, even when I don't want to hear it. And I appreciate those who tell me the facts to help me be better, not tear me down. Early in my career, I had a supervisor named Tom who reviewed my work and approved it before it became final. I still recall sitting in Tom's cubicle and discussing my work. Tom would give me pointers on how some items could be improved. He would question me on findings where perhaps I did not document them as well as I could. He taught me how to be precise and pay attention to little details. But what I remember most is not only how much I learned from Tom's honest feedback but how much I enjoyed learning from him. I did not fret about going to his office to review my work. He did not yell, he was calm, and he made it a good experience. And I knew Tom was correct in his assessments—most of the time. But even when I disagreed, it was not a negative for me. I learned a lot from Tom, and he helped prepare me for future leadership roles.

I want you to become the best, most effective leader you can be, and over the following chapters, I'll share some of the essential qualities that every great leader needs to have. You may feel uncomfortable as you move out of your comfort zone into the challenging but rewarding reality of leadership. This is a normal and necessary part of the process. You might find that some of the qualities required of leaders may take more time than others to fully implement into your leadership role. Don't lose sight of what you are working towards. You will have to change some of your regular habits to move from where you are to where you want to be. Becoming a leader is a challenging task, but I know you can do it. Nothing good in life ever comes without a lot of effort.

Santa isn't here, but don't let that deter you. Instead of waiting for Santa, be determined that you will achieve success by applying principles of leadership that work. Be determined that you can achieve anything if you put your mind and heart to work for it. So, let's get started. And let's start where you might not think we should begin—and that's with you.

Chapter 2
Lessons in Reality
Key takeaway and applied knowledge

Take it Further: Consider how the chapter relates to your current events and your expectations of quick success.

Chapter 3

IS THAT TRUE?

Lessons in Integrity

When I stepped into a leadership position with the federal government, my new boss gave me a piece of advice that has never once failed me in over thirty years of being a leader. A twenty-year veteran of the Ohio State Highway Patrol, this guy knew his stuff. He was the type who could get in your face and make life very uncomfortable for people who made him mad. So when he called me into his office one day, I was ready to listen. He told me, "Tell me the truth, don't lie to me. I can forgive mistakes, but I can't forget deception." My boss knew I was going to make mistakes as a leader. Making mistakes is inevitable.

But instead of trying to cover them up through deception—however harmless it may seem—I needed to own up to my mistakes. And that's the way it was. I never once lied to him and he came to trust me wholeheartedly. When he left the agency years later, he advocated for my promotion.

Telling the truth is a foundational principle that you must possess in order to be a good leader. It sounds like such a simple thing to do, but you would be surprised how often this is abused in the workplace. A lot of bosses tend to think that they are smarter than their employees. They think they can save face and their reputations by deceiving their subordinates without detection. But however hard they try, this strategy always fails. Employees will always find out the truth—and quickly.

"Telling the truth is a foundational principle that you must possess in order to be a good leader. It sounds like such a simple thing to do, but you would be surprised how often this is abused in the workplace."

As a leader, your actions, or lack thereof, affect the actions of your employees. If you lie to them about anything, no matter how small the deception may seem, it will slowly erode their confidence in you. You will quickly find yourself in a poisoned atmosphere filled with distrustful employees. It's like trying to grow a healthy plant in bad soil. No matter how much time and energy you spend tending to it, nothing good will grow because the foundation is bad. You will never inspire the best in your employees and cultivate a healthy team environment if you're dishonest. While spinning the truth may seem easy in the moment, it will only multiply your problems and cause you nothing but regret. And once the fire of your own deception begins to burn it is difficult to extinguish. You can't rebuild your reputation overnight.

True leadership involves trust. There's no shortcut around it or substitute for it. Honesty creates a positive atmosphere that inspires your employees to do—and be—their best. When your employees know they can fully trust your word, they will have faith in you as a leader. And your example of honesty will in turn, inspire your employees to be truthful with you. Some of the finest people I've supervised were the most honest. When they told me something, I believed them. When they explained why they did something, I believed them. Why did I believe them? Over time, they always told me the truth. I made it a practice to always be honest with my employees, and in turn, my employees were honest with me. And these employees tended to be the highest performers. Honesty matters and it manifests itself in numerous ways. As a leader, one of the best feelings is talking to an employee and knowing they are being rock-solid honest with you. If you want people to follow you, be truthful with them. This isn't rocket science—being truthful works, and it works wonderfully.

If being honest is so great, why do some leaders not tell the truth? Didn't they learn in elementary school that honesty is always the best policy? There are a lot of reasons why leaders are not always honest, and all of them stem from poor management approaches.

Sometimes leaders are not truthful because they don't want to face the challenges that honesty involves. No matter who you are, telling the truth is going to be uncomfortable at times, especially if you have to convey negative information to your employees. It hurts to tell someone they didn't get the promotion they were so hoping for. It's uncomfortable to tell someone their work needs improvement. Some employees will take offense and hold a grudge. Some of them may even quit. Faced with these outcomes, some leaders choose to shortcut the truth. But there will be employees who will take your words to heart and improve, benefiting you and your organization. Building credibility with your employees means being honest with them, no matter how difficult or uncomfortable that may be at times. The pain of being honest is short-lived, while the benefits to you and your employees will continue for years.

Some leaders don't tell the truth because they don't want to make their employees feel bad. They think a little misdirection can soften a situation so nobody's feelings are hurt. After all, what's the harm? Maybe an employee didn't give a good presentation and they ask you how they did. Maybe someone didn't get that promotion and they ask you why they weren't selected. Maybe an employee's report was not well-researched and had poor analysis. You don't want to hurt their feelings, right? No matter how well-intentioned this approach may seem, you will never make people feel good when you are dishonest with them. Not being truthful to make an employee feel good in the moment is not helpful once they find out the truth. And when they do, they will assume you're hiding other things from them as well. You will never make things better by being dishonest with your employees. Ignoring facts and downplaying results will only make things worse. If an employee is not performing up to par you must confront it in a truthful but graceful manner. Employees will never know how to improve if you don't tell them.

And some leaders are not fully truthful because they just want to be admired. They don't want to say anything negative to their employees for fear they won't be liked afterward. These leaders make the fatal mistake of believing that being liked is more important than getting better results. This causes them to accept mediocre work and look the other way while their employees fail to achieve their best. Being liked is not what you should seek in a leadership position. Now, I'm not saying a leader should be a jerk and be hated; that will never yield successful results. However, if you want to be an effective leader, you must seek to be respected rather than liked.

> *"I'm not saying a leader should be a jerk and be hated; that will never yield successful results. However, if you want to be an effective leader, you must seek to be respected rather than liked."*

Honesty is not always going to make other people happy. I remember an employee who took great offense at me for giving him honest feedback about his mediocre performance. I was gentle and kind in my feedback and was trying to help him do better. The same will happen to you at times when you give honest feedback. But that's okay because a leader's job is to get results, and the only way to achieve great results is by holding high standards and challenging employees to meet those standards. One cannot allow mediocrity to rule in the workplace; it's far too contagious. What you let one employee get away with, you must let everyone get away with. That's not the path to success. That is the path to ruin. Employees respect a leader who holds them responsible and ensures results are achieved. They respond to good leadership that helps them be better at what they do. And they love seeing success, especially when they respond to their boss's challenge.

Being honest with employees is necessary to help them improve their skills. One employee I supervised, Sue, volunteered to present at a trucking association meeting. She was new to the office and was clearly excited about the opportunity to speak at a public event. I'm always pleased to see such enthusiasm in my employees, so I readily gave her my full support to attend and speak. In the weeks leading up to the event, I reviewed some basic concepts of presenting with her to make sure she was fully prepared. I knew from previous presentations I had given that presenting to the trucking industry as a representative of the government is no walk in the park. There is always someone in the audience ready to disrupt and challenge your presentation. But Sue assured me she had everything under control and was ready to go.

On the day of the event, Sue confidently walked up to the podium and began her speech. She began by talking about the safety regulations and how the companies attending this event should comply. She was doing great. She was enthusiastic, smiling, looking at the audience, and quoting the applicable regulations from memory. She was about ten minutes into her thirty-minute presentation when it happened ... a person raised their hand with a question. Sue stopped her presentation and kindly asked the person to speak. But it was not a question that Sue received. It was a disgruntled trucker contesting what she had stated from the podium. No matter how Sue responded, the trucker kept on complaining. It was no longer a presentation but a gripe session.

Unfortunately, Sue didn't handle it well. Panicked, she frantically called me up to the stage from the back of the room to respond to the trucker's complaints. "How did I do?" she asked me hesitantly afterward. "Well ..." I responded, "here's what you can learn from this." Rather than reprimanding or disparaging her, I used this as an opportunity to teach her how to handle these types of individuals during presentations. She learned from it and went on to do well in her career. The key? I was honest and supportive in the feedback I gave to her.

Telling the truth doesn't mean you have to be mean-spirited or condescending to others. You can be honest without destroying someone's confidence. Nothing about telling the truth requires you to insult or intentionally hurt someone. It's about helping others, not hurting them. If one of your employees makes a mistake—as my employee did in her presentation—and you do not address it, then your employee will never overcome that mistake and improve. It will only continue to harm them and may even prevent them from achieving better opportunities. Being honest and supportive in your feedback to employees is about helping them become the best employee they can be. It will help them get the promotion next time. It will help them learn how to present more effectively next time. It will help them write a better report with better analysis next time. But these results will only happen if you are honest in a way that seeks to uplift, not tear down.

"Telling the truth doesn't mean you have to be mean-spirited or condescending to others. You can be honest without destroying someone's confidence."

You shortchange your employees if you do not tell them the truth about their performance. As a leader, you are in a position to help employees see their flaws and correct them. If you don't actively engage in this work, you— and your employee—will see the same mistakes re-appear over and over again. This will hurt your organization in the short term and will greatly hurt your employee in the long term. Your job as a leader is to get results. And you get great results by helping your employees be the best they can be by telling them the truth in a graceful, supportive manner.

When you help your employees become better workers, you make yourself better too. When they achieve better results, you get better results too. When they output more, you output more. Your job and its results are directly related to your subordinates. That's why it's so important to help your employees succeed. If they fail, you will fail too. If they don't reach their goals, you won't reach yours either. If their work is sloppy, yours is too. When I first became a leader, my goal was to make every one of my employees succeed because I knew it would translate into my success.

What about the times when you shouldn't share information with employees? There will undoubtedly be times when you must exercise careful discretion in determining how much information to share with employees. Maybe certain information is for supervisors' eyes only. Or maybe a big announcement will be made soon and you aren't at liberty to share it until then. Maybe you know something that involves personal information that can't be shared. In these situations, you can still be honest and upfront with employees while at the same time not sharing the information that's been entrusted to you. You are not required to always share everything you know when an employee asks; there's a big difference between lying and being discreet. But if you decide not to share certain information with your employees, it is always better to be honest about it. A polite "I can't share that at this time" or "That isn't something I can discuss" will go a long way to retaining your employees' trust even though you have to withhold information from them sometimes. I've done this many times and can tell you that most employees understand the good intentions behind this. They appreciate the fact that I'm honest with them. They know there are some questions that I can't answer, and that's okay as long as it is done in a way that maintains your integrity and honesty with your employees.

***

Honesty is a necessity in leadership, even in the most difficult circumstances. Early in my career with the government, I was a Federal Safety Investigator, which meant it was my job to visit trucking companies and look for violations of federal truck safety regulations. It might sound simple, but sometimes it was like walking into a lion's den. I conducted my reviews alone, surrounded by company officials who at times scrutinized my movements and bombarded me with questions. And some of them quite frankly didn't want me there. "Are we meeting the regulations? Are you finding anything wrong?" they asked constantly. "How's our safety rating? Will it be satisfactory?" I understood their worries. The safety rating is very important to trucking businesses and it is public information, so a bad rating can severely hurt their business. What would you say if asked these questions? Would you lie and say everything is okay to make these officials relax, only to hand them a copy of your report detailing their numerous violations? Would you not write the violations because you felt bad for the company? How would you handle it?

When I found violations during my reviews and knew the company would receive a penalty and a lower safety rating as a result, I told the company the truth. I responded to their questions by politely asking them to let me finish my review and assured them that we would discuss my findings together. At the end of each review, I explained each of my findings to company officials, showing them why it was considered a violation and how they could correct it. I let them know how their company's violations affected safety and why it was important for them to improve. I also let them know, when appropriate, that they could expect to receive a penalty for their violations. Were they happy with what I had to say? No. Never. But in most cases, company officials thanked me for being honest with them. Many of them told me it was a breath of fresh air for them to be told the truth by a government representative.

You see, these trucking companies knew the truth before I walked into their businesses to conduct my reviews. Most knew they were not complying as they should, so my findings were never much of a surprise. But here's the key: I gave company officials negative information with respect and humility. I didn't preach down to them, and

I never insulted them. I maintained their dignity and respect while conveying truthful information. This approach even helped the agency further achieve its goals, as few of my investigations were challenged. Being truthful even in challenging circumstances is possible as long as your intent is not to belittle but to help others improve.

Now after reading most of this chapter you may be saying, "Come on, Steve, I'm not like that." "I don't mislead others." "This does not apply to me." Well, let me give you a few final thoughts on how to remain honest in your leadership duties.

First, be careful not to exaggerate accomplishments. When reporting something you or your team did, be straightforward with the results. There is a tendency to puff up results, whether they be sales numbers or the outcome of new projects attempted. I could also call this accentuating the positive. Keep it simple—report the actual facts. Share what went well and what could be improved. When you do this it forms a habit in you to critically examine what you are reporting for accuracy and honesty. And in the end it makes your programs better because you objectively looked at them for their results. When folks constantly exaggerate their accomplishments, it leads to poor work outcomes. They convince themselves that they are doing better than they really are and in the process, they don't critically assess the truth. In the end it comes back to harm them. Saying good things about yourself or what you accomplished is great! In fact, it's encouraged. Celebrating your accomplishments and being proud of what you've achieved is important, and I love to do it myself. But make sure when you do you don't go overboard on what is real and factual.

"First, be careful not to exaggerate accomplishments. When reporting something you or your team did, be straightforward with the results... I could also call this accentuating the positive."

Another way where people can slip is by telling half-truths. This is where you tell one part of the story, but leave out the other. For example, "our sales numbers were great this month, look how well my team did." What you did not say was that most of that was from a few companies and not overall growth. Do you see the issue here? It's easy to fall on this one because many times we don't want to include "other" information that is not as pleasant to report.

It erodes one's credibility when it is discovered that not all the facts were presented. I don't know about you, but I dislike it greatly when someone only gives me half the facts. Because half the facts is a lie, plain and simple. When the other half that I did not disclose gets in the open, guess who is going to look like a fool? Me. And my boss is not going to be happy. Because when you give half-truths you are deceitful and nobody likes to be deceived. Give the whole story and be up-front about it.

The last recommendation is don't deny what you did. Everything you do as a leader can come under scrutiny—every decision, every word, every action. Own up to it. If you did something then stand by it, even if it was wrong. There is a story from World War II that involved a very powerful U.S. admiral and one of his commanders. The commander sent one of his ships into a port under the guise that it needed repair. He was supposed to get the admiral's permission to send the ship into port, but decided to take matters into his own hands.

The admiral found out about it and he called the commander into his office the next time he was in port. The commander was nervous because he knew why he really sent the ship into port without the admiral's permission. The real reason was not to repair the ship. It was not due to war damage. It was not to fix a non-working item on the ship. The real reason he sent one of the ships under his command into port was, well, it was a booze run. That's right—a booze run. He sent the ship in during wartime to pick up liquor for his men. And he deceived the admiral in the process. And now the admiral wanted to see him. The commander was worried, he thought his career was over. He decided before seeing the admiral that he was going to own it. And he did.

The admiral point-blank asked him why he sent the ship to port without his permission. The commander told him the truth. It was a booze run. The admiral was taken aback. "You mean, you sent that ship down there for booze?" the admiral asked.[1] The commander responded, "Yes." You see, the admiral also believed that men in combat, whose lives could be taken away at any moment, deserved a few drinks when they were off duty. He forgave the commander and did not hold it against him. The admiral I'm writing about was William "Bull" Halsey. You'll hear more about this great admiral later in this book.

A leader owns up to their decisions, both good and bad. And I can tell you that I also owned up to some poor decisions in my career. My supervisors always showed me grace when I did. Always. And I've done the same for others. People who tell the truth are like a breath of fresh air. And sometimes there may be consequences for poor decisions. That's okay. I always believed it was better to live with integrity because that is who I am. I didn't deceive my superiors or my team. That's a leader.

As a leader, being honest is not optional—it's mandatory. You will find that something as simple as telling the truth is going to pay many dividends for you at the professional level and even more so at a personal level. Not only will telling the truth benefit your organization, but it will also relieve you of stress and cultivate a healthy work

---

1   John Wukovits, Admiral "Bull" Halsey, 2010, p. 141

environment. And as you make a practice of being hon-est, it'll become much easier to continue. It will become second nature in all of your dealings to the point where you won't even have to think about it! Remember what your mom taught you when you were a kid—don't lie, and always tell the truth. Everything else I cover in this book is built on this one powerful principle. Now, it's time to move on and get to work.

Chapter 3
Lessons in Integrity
Key takeaway and applied knowledge

Take it Further: What values did you identify with? What do they mean to you? How have you experienced them in your workplace?

Chapter 4

NO SUBSTITUTE

Lessons in Hard Work

I arrived at work to find pots and pans stacked three feet high in the sink. They were filthy, with all kinds of left-over food cooked into them. I dug through what felt like a mountain of dishes so that I could get the water running. Frantically I began washing and scrubbing by hand every pot, pan, and plate the cooks had used in the kitchen that morning—and would be using again soon for the dinner rush. I washed and scrubbed as fast as my hands could move while more pots and pans were thrown in my sink with a *"Watch out—hot"* warning. Two hours later, I finally began to see the bottom of the sink. I sighed, feeling a wave of relief wash over me. It was short-lived.

The dinner time rush began, and so did the non-stop work of scrubbing, rinsing, and repeating. As the workload increased, a common phrase from my supervisor could be heard: *"Time to kick in."* I worked at a breathtaking pace for the next five hours, scrubbing and rinsing every pot and pan in sight. At ten o'clock, the work finally slowed. The final kitchen clean-up could begin. After another two hours, I headed home, completely exhausted. I would do it all over again next weekend. And so went my high school job.

That dishwashing job taught me that things don't come easy. I learned that I better be ready to kick it into high gear when called upon. This work ethic has served me well in my leadership career. A strong work ethic is required if you want to lead others. As the leader, you set the example. You can never ask others to do what you won't do. Remember what we talked about at the beginning of this book: Santa Claus is gone—*finito*. If you want something, you have to earn it. And as a supervisor of employees, you must be willing to work hard, long, and smart.

I'm a history buff. I love learning about men and women throughout the ages who overcame obstacles to become great leaders. As I read books about various events and historical figures, I've learned a lot about successful leaders from all walks of life, including industry, government, and the military. These leaders, some of whom you will read about later in this book, have a simple yet powerful trait in common. It's something that cannot be taught but is essential to successfully lead others: a strong work ethic. If you study any great leader throughout history, you will find the same. These leaders are hard workers for a reason—it's necessary. There are no free passes or exemptions here. You will never achieve the results you want to see without it. It is one of the foundational keys to being an effective leader.

*"If you study any great leader
throughout history, you will find the same.
These leaders are hard workers for a
reason—it's necessary."*

I've also worked with individuals in my career whom I considered to be outstanding leaders. And again, one recurring trait I could identify in each one was that they all had a superb work ethic. They were hard workers, led by example, and inspired me to work harder. I was surprised how often I noticed this trait in what I considered a good leader. It took me some time to connect the clues with what I read from history and what I met in real life. This was a common trait in good leadership. This was something that had to be there. There is no substitute for it. And the demands and trials of a leader require it for success.

What is a strong work ethic? You might be asking. It isn't easy to define, but let me tell you what it isn't. A strong work ethic is not about seeing who can work the longest. It isn't about how much time you spend at the office. It has nothing to do with who works most weekends. A strong work ethic is about what you are willing to do to get the job done. It's kicking into high gear when the circumstances require it. It's staying up late and getting up early when the task requires it. It's being available until the job is done. It's traveling back-to-back weeks away from family to fix a problem or encourage employees. It is working all day and then into the night to solve a problem. It's dropping what you are doing on a Sunday and spending hours responding to a critical situation. A leader does these things because that's who they are. They accept that hard work and sacrifice go with the territory. And they are not afraid of it. And they are driven to succeed despite the costs.

When I started my career with the government, my office didn't have a computer program to record and track safety complaints from the public made against trucking companies. Back in those days, everything was done by hand. My supervisor came to me and asked if I knew how to write a program that would automatically track all of the complaints we received. I was honest with him; I had no idea how to write such a program. But I told him that if I had a programming book, I'm sure I could learn how to do it.

A few days later, my supervisor returned with a Dbase programming book for me to learn how to write the program he wanted. I started going into the office on weekends to use the computer there to write my code. I was so committed to learning the process and finishing the project that I didn't even mind working the extra hours. On one of those weekends, my supervisor came into the office and was surprised to see me sitting at the computer, completely immersed in the code I was working on. I made an impression on him that day. A few years later, he recommended me for a promotion. It was my first promotion to a management position in the government.

My supervisor never asked me to work on Saturdays, but I did. I didn't work the extra hours to impress him; I did it because I wanted to accomplish the goal he had set before me. I wanted to be proud of writing the first Dbase complaint-tracking program for my office. I wanted to succeed. And I did. Going the extra mile set me apart from my coworkers and enabled me to move to bigger and better things within the agency. The promotions I enjoyed time and again throughout my career were all due to applying the combined work ethic of commitment and perseverance.

> *"My supervisor never asked me to work on Saturdays, but I did. I didn't work the extra hours to impress him; I did it because I wanted to accomplish the goal he had set before me."*

Again, the challenge of leadership demands a strong work ethic to succeed. You will face challenges that require not only skill and thoughtfulness but hard work to complete. Whether you must meet deadlines, production goals, address customer concerns or deal with an employee issue, there will be countless times when you must "kick in" to get the work done.

If you've ever worked in the government, you know that budget cuts are a fact of life. During one such round of cuts, I was tasked with handling two other jobs in addition to my own. A key management position in my office had been vacant for over a year and a half, yet we couldn't afford to fill the position due to budget constraints. To make matters worse, my secretary, who handled all administrative issues for the office, left for another job. As the leader, it was my job to keep everything running smoothly. It ended up being one of the most challenging periods in my career.

Day after day, I completed the work of three positions and periodically rotated other employees in to assist on specific projects and tasks. I returned home each night exhausted, only to do the same thing again the next day. Yet the thought of quitting or leaving the work unfinished never entered my mind. I knew I was going to get the job done somehow because I was responsible for the success of the office. I was not going to fail without putting up a fight. After months of long hours and hard work, the positions were finally filled, and I returned to my one full-time job.

As a leader, there will be times when it's on you—and you alone—to fix a relationship, save a client, or increase sales. If one engine fails, you still have to keep the plane flying. You must approach leadership expecting things to go awry and your plans to fall

through. And when you're facing a time where you need to kick it into high gear, having the right attitude is key to successfully managing a demanding workload. Be willing to work harder than you ever have before to succeed. Be ready to do whatever it takes to make your team, unit, and office successful. Set an example to your employees that you will work harder than what you ever expect from them.

*** *** ***

People that join the U.S. Military know they're in for a lot of hard work. When I volunteered to join the Marines, I knew that I was facing a tough road ahead of me. I had read about their legendary training center at Parris Island, S.C., so I had some idea of what awaited me when I arrived. It was more difficult than anything I'd imagined, and it never got much better.

When I was in the field with my infantry unit, we were constantly moving and exposed to all the elements that the hot, humid South Carolina weather had to offer. Insects were everywhere, and we never got enough food or sleep. Wet, cold, tired, smelly, you name it, we kept moving. The constant call to keep going—whether day or night—never ceased. There was little downtime, and we were continually challenged and pushed to our mental and physical limits. Things did not get easier after I completed training. Grueling days and nights of war games awaited me. I was so exhausted on one such mission that I fell asleep on my feet in the pouring rain. The helicopters sent for us never arrived. I woke up as I hit the ground, then almost did it again!

Nobody joins the Marines for an easy, fun time. They join for the love of the challenge. If it were easy, more people would do it! Being a leader in the Marines meant that after a long day, I usually went to bed last and got up first. While others were in their tents for the night, I ensured everyone had chow and water for the next day. As my squad relaxed, I planned, got the supplies my unit needed, and met with other leaders for further orders. I didn't get chow until my squad did, and I always ensured they had water before I got any. A leader always goes further than those they supervise and never asks more of others than they are willing to give.

> *"Nobody joins the Marines for an easy, fun time. They join for the love of the challenge. If it were easy, more people would do it! Being a leader in the Marines meant that after a long day, I usually went to bed last and got up first."*

As a leader, you set the example. Your employees watch you more than you think. They see what time you arrive and what time you leave. They see how long you take for lunch and if you stay late to finish the job. They see all this and more. So what? You might be thinking, *If I'm the boss, I should be able to do what I want.* It's tempting to feel this way, but it's a mistake. Your employees receive their direction on how to behave from you. Even without saying a word, you communicate to your employees. Your actions speak much louder and are remembered longer than anything you say.

If you want your employees to work hard and put in a good day's work each day, you need to do the same. If you ask them to stay late to finish an assignment or go the extra mile on a project, you also need to. You can't expect your employees to be timely if you aren't. It's difficult to inspire strong work habits in your employees if you are not providing an example of the behaviors you want to see. Employees quickly lose respect for a leader they consider a hypocrite, and they'll begin to mimic your poor work habits. If you find yourself in a situation like this, don't worry; change is possible, and it starts with you.

The positive side is that employees will also mimic your strong work habits. When you come into work on time, the message is sent—be on time. And when you work overtime to finish an assignment, you're communicating to your employees to put in the same effort when it's required of them. It's more difficult for employees to complain when their boss works just as long and hard as them. This is called leading by example. And it's an effective way to inspire hard work and good habits in employees.

I had an employee, James, who was new to my office, and I noticed he began to show up late each morning. Now, I can let this slide once or twice. We all have days when we wake up late or have car problems, or our kids have issues getting off to school. It's a fact of life. But I can't excuse a bad habit. James kept arriving late morning after morning, so I called him into my office to discuss the problem. "Well ..." he stammered, "traffic varies each day which causes me to run late." *Traffic? Really?* I almost laughed out loud. "I deal with traffic every morning too, James," I told him. "And yet I still manage to get to work on time." I could see his jaw starting to drop as he sensed where I was going with this. "Expect traffic variance each day and plan accordingly to get to work on time. No excuses. If I can do it, so can you."

James was never late to work again. He began arriving fifteen minutes early each day after our talk. When one of the other employees asked James why he was always early, he replied that he didn't want to be late. When your actions align with your work habit, you become highly persuasive. It would have been difficult for me to correct James if I wasn't showing up promptly for work. Since I provided a pattern of the behavior I wanted him to model, he put aside his excuses and followed my example.

A leader must set a good example for all employees, including other supervisors. When I was a division administrator, I required my subordinate supervisors to monitor their phones after work hours in case something urgent arose that required immediate attention. Sometimes they needed to get a hold of me after hours—and I always responded promptly. My phone never left my side no matter where I was; even at home, my phone was always within range. What message do you think I sent my subordinate supervisors when I responded to their emails on nights and weekends? I showed my employees that I wasn't asking them to do anything I wasn't already doing. I didn't expect more from them than I did from myself.

When your employees see your behavior, they get the message and respect you for it. You are sending your employees the wrong message if you require them to work late nights and be available 24/7 if you are not holding yourself to that same standard. You can't ask others to sacrifice if you won't. Show your employees that you do everything you ask of them—and more.

Being a leader also comes with stress and sacrifice, not only for you but also for your family. I moved my family to another state four times to pursue promotions. I've traveled extensively throughout my career with the federal government, sometimes for weeks back-to-back. Traveling for work added stress to my personal life, and I lost time with my family and kids. It wasn't easy being away for all those weeks that my job required; it was also difficult for my family. But sacrifice is part of the job. Those sacrifices paid off for me with numerous career promotions and financial rewards. Looking back now, I'm glad I did it, but it was not an easy road. It never is.

> *"Being a leader also comes with stress and sacrifice, not only for you but also for your family."*

Recently, a colleague of mine was on a national call sharing her wisdom about leadership. She started as a secretary in Indiana and worked for the same agency as I did. Her story is one of hard work and sacrifice. She moved to Ohio, where she was promoted numerous times, eventually being put in charge of the Ohio office. After that, she was again promoted and moved her family to the Baltimore area. She received more promotions and achieved outstanding success with the agency. In front of our colleagues across the country, she spoke about the sacrifices leadership requires. She described the challenges of her first promotion and moving her family to pursue better opportunities. Her story was personal to me. I was the one who promoted her to her first management position in the agency. I related to her sacrifices, as some were similar to mine. Eventually, through her determination, hard work, and sacrifice, she became one of the agency's top leaders.

Leadership is not about working the most hours or spending the longest time away from family. I'm certainly not advocating that you need to work 24/7 to be a good leader. That's not good for your mental or physical

health and will ruin personal relationships with loved ones. That isn't what a good work ethic is about. A strong work ethic sets an example for those you supervise to follow. It demonstrates effective leadership and shows others how to get the job done no matter what it takes. It sometimes calls you to "kick in" to get the work done. A strong work ethic helps the organization make it through tough times. It's willing to sacrifice to get ahead and sees you through to success and promotions.

This work ethic I'm talking about is already within you. You have what it takes to give this outstanding level of effort. You have what it takes to inspire others to work hard and do a good job. Get ready to use it. Your leadership role may not require you to work excessive hours, travel frequently, or work every weekend. But it will demand something more from you than you are used to giving. Make sure you approach leadership prepared to sacrifice and work harder than you ever have before. There is no substitute for it.

Now let's focus on a topic you probably haven't heard much about lately. I didn't want to bring this up, but you need it more than you think.

Chapter 4
Lessons in Hard Work
Key takeaway and applied knowledge

Take it Further: Take a moment to reflect on the chapter's message. What message does your work ethic send to your employees?

Chapter 5

DON'T RUN OUT OF THIS

Lessons in Patience

Recently I visited northwest California on a camping trip. During my time there, I saw one of the tallest trees in the world. Known as the Giant Tree (creative, huh?), this redwood tree stands 363 feet tall and has a circumference of fifty-three feet! I stood in awe at the tree's base, looking up at its enormous height towering over every other tree nearby. I marveled at the strength of its root system to hold up such a colossal tree in heavy winds and intense storms. As I stood there looking up at it, I felt like an ant, so incredibly small next to this beautiful giant. And as I looked up, a thought entered my mind, as it probably has for countless others who had stood there before me: "How long did it take this tree to grow so tall?" The answer was much longer than I could imagine. It reminded me that things take time—a lot of time—to grow, and the bigger they are, the more time it takes.

It's time to talk about something that is no longer popular. In fact, many believe it's a bad word. When you use this word, you will more than likely receive a dirty look in return. *You can't be serious*, people might tell you. *Come on—nobody does that anymore.* In our world of instant messaging, instant shopping, and instant delivery, this word seems out of place. So why am I even bringing it up? Without this word, you can't build anything long-lasting. Without it, you can't survive the setbacks and brick walls you will inevitably run into as a leader. You won't achieve great things with others without this word. It's indispensable for success, and since I want you to succeed as a leader, we have to talk about this unpopular word.

The word I'm talking about is ... well, be patient now, and I'll get to it. Did you catch it? It's the P-word: Patience. As a leader, you must exercise patience. You need to be patient with people and situations that don't lend themselves to easy fixes. You need to be patient when everyone else is in panic mode. As a leader, you will regularly encounter people, things, and situations that you want to change immediately. But be careful because while some things can change quickly, many others cannot. Constantly attempting to change what requires time and patience to resolve will drive you, those around you, and those you supervise crazy. Often, you'll end up hurting yourself and failing at your job.

You have undoubtedly heard the phrase, "Rome was not built in a day." Rome was one of the greatest empires in history and lasted for almost one thousand years. Strong and powerful, it dominated the world. Of course, it wasn't built in a day. Giant trees that stand over 360 feet tall don't grow in a day. Great things take time and lots of it. The same is true for raising children. If you have kids, you know it takes money, housing, and food—the basics of life—to raise them. But most importantly, it takes time and patience. Marriages require the same. Try building a successful relationship without patience. It won't work. Try raising kids that grow up to be great individuals that love and respect you as a parent. You can't do it without patience. Beautiful relationships with a spouse, child, or friend require patience as the foundational building block to their success. The most incredible things ever built on this earth required time and patience to reach their full potential. And the same goes for you as a leader.

One definition of patience is "the capacity to accept or tolerate delay, trouble or suffering, without getting angry or upset."[1] Contrary to popular belief, patience isn't passive. It's not sitting on your hands all day waiting for something great to happen. Patience is deliberative planning and thoughtful decision-making. It does not signal giving up, giving in, or quitting; instead, it is an active movement toward a goal. It isn't laziness or capitulation but a continual effort to overcome and succeed. Patience is an investment in success.

And it is needed when dealing with humans. As much as we might want them to, employees don't operate like machines. You can't expect them to work nonstop and produce fantastic results 100 percent of the time. If you want to improve their results, you can—but it takes time. Some leaders just run their employees over with brute

---

1   Oxford Languages via Google

force. This happens in relationships too, when one side loses all patience and continually resorts to hurtful tactics. And yet, success is not attained by these methods. The casualties pile up. The damage done can destroy careers, goodwill, relationships, and families forever. There is a better way to deal with issues and overcome obstacles in your workplace and your relationships. And the more it's worth to you, the more investment is required.

"Contrary to popular belief, patience isn't passive. It's not sitting on your hands all day waiting for something great to happen."

When I was the division administrator of California, my office took issue with the state for not completing enough safety audits of trucking companies. A safety audit was a review performed on a company that recently registered with the agency. The state had a contract with our office to conduct these reviews. However, the state got behind on conducting them. A backlog of audits continued to grow until hundreds of audits were piled up. Yet, the state seemed unable to fix the issue.

I called a meeting with the leadership of the state agency to discuss the issue. Do you know what they said? "We're maxed out," they told me. "We can't do any more audits. We don't like this program to begin with, so you're lucky we're even doing the ones we've done." Now imagine you are in my shoes. How would you respond? Would you slam your fist on the desk and tell them that's unacceptable? Would you tell them they are under contract and have to do it? Hundreds of audits are behind schedule. What's your plan at this meeting right now to solve the issue? Let me give you a hint. If you don't exercise patience right now, these state officials could walk out and quit the contract. And because they do other important work for you under contract, they could potentially throw that away too. If that happens, your bosses will lose total faith in your ability to lead. You're in a no-win situation. Time to panic? Nope. It's time for patience.

So how did I respond in that meeting? I quickly realized this situation could not be solved in an instant. It wasn't going to be solved with anger or condescension. Instead, I decided to rely on a few simple steps that seem so basic yet are so powerful when combined. And yep, you guessed it, they all revolve around that unpopular word—patience.

First, I listened. I know, I know—you've heard that preached to you a million times, right? Listening is a key action that will help you in difficult situations. As frustrated as I was with the problem, I didn't interrupt them during the meeting, I didn't judge them, and I didn't debate points with them. It's imperative when listening to someone else that you hold your fire—even when you disagree with what they say. When I was a safety investigator conducting inspections of trucking companies, I was trained to just let company officials talk. They'll always tell you more when you let them talk freely than by asking yes or no questions. Even better, listening to others comes across as a sign of respect. Company officials began to like me just because I spent time listening to what they had to say.

I applied this same strategy in the meeting with these California state officials. I started the discussion with a brief overview, and then I just let them talk. I didn't have to remind them of the problem—they already knew it. I didn't have to tell them how important this was or why it was so urgent—they already knew. As they finished speaking, I asked clarifying questions to confirm I understood their point of view. Such questions are critical to ensure every-one is on the same page and can move forward toward results.

As I listened to the state officials' explanation for the backlog of safety audits, they told me they couldn't force their employees to complete them. "Technically, we're not required to complete these audits, so we're doing you a favor by completing what we can," they told me. That wasn't the answer I wanted to hear. Yet I relied on patience to help me find common ground with them and under-stand their side of this issue. "I understand," I told them. "We have employee rules ourselves that make it difficult to get all of our work done at times. I appreciate the effort you and your team have been making to complete what you can." I could tell they were taken aback by my lack of anger or visible frustration. Almost immediately, they let down their defenses, and we began to talk back and forth in a more friendly, honest manner.

As we talked, the state officials said something that floored me. "I guess in other words, our employees can be lazy sometimes," they told me. They may have been joking, but I couldn't believe what I had heard. Coming into this meeting, they never blamed their own employees for the pileup of safety audits. But by listening to them and showing them that I understood their situation, these officials knew they could trust me. As a result, they became more honest with me. You have to understand the problem others are facing to truly be able to address an issue head-on and resolve it effectively. The patience I showed these officials had opened the door between us just a tiny crack, and now I was ready to take the next step.

Second, I identified solutions. Now that the state officials trusted me, I could focus my efforts on the task at hand: getting more safety audits completed. After listening to others explain their understanding of the problem, the next step in patience is to ask them for the solution. You read that right—ask them for the solution. It sounds way too easy, but trust me, it is a critical aspect of building trust and collaboration with others. Once these state officials explained their side of the issue, I asked them to provide a few solutions. I didn't suggest one because I wanted their input on how to solve the problem. People appreciate when you include them in the problem-solving process, especially when they know you hold the keys to resolution.

You see, I couldn't impose my solution on them. If I had sat in that conference room and told them to comply with my solution or else, they would have abruptly left the meeting. Instead, I asked them how we could address this issue together. They responded with a couple of suggestions. And surprisingly, one of those suggestions was to get their employees to do more work. I could never have told them to do that without inciting anger and derision. These officials had to arrive at that conclusion on their own, and once they did, things finally started moving. We came to an agreement on how best to split up tasks and assignments related to safety audits. When they noticed I was willing and committed to helping they became more dedicated to the matter at hand. Breakthroughs like this are only possible with patience. But continued collaboration, teamwork, and problem-solving take time—and more patience.

Finally, I kept advancing toward the goal. Big problems don't get solved overnight. The key to progress is keeping your eyes on the goal and moving toward it. The state officials and I had made a great start toward resolving the pile-up of safety audits. But it would take several meetings, agreements, and some program changes to finally get the program firing on all cylinders. We began meeting during lunch on Fridays to check up with each other. Only about ten minutes of our hour-long meetings were spent talking about progress on the safety audits; the rest was spent on friendly chats. Each session resulted in more trust and friendship and then ... problem solved. The number of audits completed by the state increased significantly, and the backlog of audits waiting for completion dwindled. The difference couldn't have been starker: from the brink of disaster to unbelievable success in less than a year, all because of patience.

> *"Big problems don't get solved overnight. The key to progress is keeping your eyes on the goal and moving toward it."*

Relying on patience when responding to complex circumstances and situations will help you achieve the results you want to see. It's been such a key to my success that I could fill this book with nothing but examples of times when patience helped me achieve great results. Patience will enable you to diffuse tense situations and address the root cause of issues. Keep at it. Don't give up. You may hit a wall for a time, but that's okay. I hit walls all the time in my line of work. But I always look on that wall for cracks to appear. And suddenly, a big issue that had been stalemated for a long time—like the safety-audit backlog—is resolved.

You may be in a situation right now where you feel like you're in neutral and not making progress. Keep your eyes and mind moving forward. Look for opportunities, changes, or anything that allows you to begin making progress on that issue. Keep asking, keep meeting and keep talking with others. Sometimes being patient in a situation is like playing defense. And I don't like playing defense. But even when I must, my mind is focused on offense and what I'm planning next. That's what great leaders do. You may be on defense for a time—we all are—but keep your mind on offense. Staying patient and looking ahead to your next moves will enable you to make big things happen and achieve outstanding results.

A little bit of patience will also help you develop good employees. Your job as a leader is to develop and help the talent below you become better at their jobs. As they get better, so will your results. And your job will get easier. But it takes time and commitment to work with them. It takes time and patience to grow them in their duties. But this is what good leaders do. And I've had the good fortune to work with some great folks I believe developed into better leaders because of my efforts. I could say the same for those who helped me grow in my career. I was always amazed to see so many of my employees become leaders in their fields beyond my expectations. I watched as they matured and eventually got promotions. I felt a sense of satisfaction knowing I was part of it. I spent time investing in their future. It was an investment that paid many dividends and provided me with personal satisfaction to witness. This is the cycle of leadership. Leaders produce other leaders who, in turn, will help create yet other leaders.

Make sure you add some patience to your skillset. The kind of patience that helps you be better and achieve bigger things. You need it not only in your professional life but personally as well. The habit of patience is not obtained overnight, so continue to work at it.

I'm frequently asked if my patience ever runs out on a problem or a person. It does, but never as soon as you might think. I've had a lot of practice over my thirty years of leadership to build up my capacity to respond to issues and people as patiently as possible. Remember, no matter how difficult the issue is, great things aren't built in a day. Big problems don't get solved overnight. It takes time to learn how to rely on patience and practice it in your day-to-day tasks and assignments, but once you do, it'll strengthen your ability to lead effectively.

Oh, by the way, the Giant Tree is estimated to be close to 1,600 years old, based on similar-size trees that fell and where the age was accurately determined. Now, there's another P-word I need to talk with you about, and it's one that you're probably more experienced with.

Chapter 5
Lessons in Patience
Key Takeaways and Applied Knowledge

Take it Further: Visit my website (MattioliSolutions.com) for more insights and training resources on how to implement this principle in your career. See my video training series: "The First 7-Steps every leader should take."

Chapter 6

A TIME FOR PANIC

Lessons in Crisis Leadership

I knew it was coming sooner or later. I studied these types of maneuvers in school, but I was taken entirely by surprise when it finally happened to me. I was piloting a Cessna 152, a small plane, with my flight instructor, Arthur, when he told me to put the nose of the plane high in the sky. That's a place the plane didn't like to go. *You can do this*, I told myself to calm my nerves. *Just like you studied*. My heart beat faster as I nervously piloted the plane upwards. The shrill beep of the stall alarm went off and steadily grew louder and louder as the plane struggled to keep moving up, up, up. Our speed decreased rapidly the higher we reached, the stall horn now blaring in my ears. All of a sudden, it happened. The plane stalled. If you are not a pilot, a stall is when the plane basically stops flying, and gravity takes over.

We became a 1,600-pound brick falling straight toward the earth! I froze, petrified. My life flashed before my eyes as we hurtled downwards. For Arthur, a World War II pilot who flew a four-engine B-24 bomber during the war, this was like a walk in the park. He sat beside me relaxed and calm as ever, while I watched in horror as the ground came closer and closer.

I was taught everything I needed to know about recovering from a stall in flight school, but now, as I panicked, I couldn't remember any of it. Arthur, help me out here! The plane was not happy, and neither was I. *What was I taught, what was I taught?* I thought frantically to myself. There's only so much time to figure it out with the ground getting closer, and panicking is just wasting time. *Think, think!* Then it all came back to me—push the stick forward, pull the power back, opposite rudder to the spin direction. Sweaty and shaky, I followed these steps and watched as the plane came back up to the horizon. We're flying again! I'm going to live another day! I breathed a huge sigh of relief and looked over at Arthur, who hadn't said one word the entire time. "Let's do another one!" he told me.

Remaining calm in times of panic is an essential trait you must learn and apply as a leader. It's particularly important when the circumstance at hand seems out of control and those around you are panicking. When everything is heading south, when the water is rising, when you can't get a break, and when nothing seems to work, staying calm allows you to think, focus, and analyze the situation. Panic creates fear and paralyzes your response. The way you approach and respond to a difficult situation cues your employees. If you panic, they will panic too. But if you stay calm and react deliberately, so will they.

Panic is defined as sudden uncontrollable fear or anxiety and often results in unwise decisions. At one time or another, we've all experienced panic. It can overcome you suddenly and without warning. Before you know it, you're in complete panic mode—frantically thinking, rushing to decisions, and making bad choices. It's bad enough to panic when nobody else is around, but what about when you are surrounded by others who are looking to you for guidance in times of trouble? Here's the key: don't stay in panic mode too long.

In leadership, panic-inducing situations will happen all the time. In my government work, a letter from a congressman could provoke panic. A bad crash on the news where the agency's oversight is questioned can send workers into panic mode. I've seen leaders, some of whom I consider to be good leaders, panic over these things too. Then there are other leaders who make a habit of panicking over the most minor, inconsequential things. Some folks just like to panic and run around like the world is ending. No matter what the situation, the world is usually not ending. Leaders often don't realize how poorly panic reflects on their leadership abilities. It's easy to get caught up in the emotions of the moment and let your fears run wild.

But such a response only conveys weakness to your employees looking to you for guidance in times of trouble.

"No matter what the situation, the world is usually not ending. Leaders often don't realize how poorly panic reflects on their leadership abilities."

Panic places your emotions in charge with your mind following their lead, clouding your judgment when you need it the most. When you panic, you send the message that things are out of control and that you don't know what to do. This is not the response you need when you face a challenging situation. Panic will not help you solve anything.

Imagine you are a passenger on a flight that's experiencing bad turbulence. All of a sudden, you hear the pilot's voice on the intercom in a nervous, panicked voice saying, "Things are not looking good, everyone." How would that make you feel? Terrified, most likely! You and everyone around you would be freaking out. This is what it's like when leaders act panicked in front of their employees. It only spreads panic throughout the organization and hinders efforts to get things under control for an effective response.

I could give you example after example of leaders in positions where we might agree they had a right to panic—but didn't. In 1988, a 737 airliner flown by TACA airlines lost power in both engines as it encountered severe thunderstorm activity heading into New Orleans from Belize. That seems like a perfect time to panic, right? Yet the pilots kept their cool and were able to glide the plane to a safe landing on a grass levee. Not one passenger was harmed.

A U.S. general during World War II faced an onslaught of German soldiers at the Battle of the Bulge. In late 1944, the German Army made one last massive assault to push the Allies back from the German homeland. The Germans were wreaking havoc and costing the Allies thousands of casualties. The battle would become the bloodiest of WWII for the American army.[1] As this U.S. general met with his top commanders to confront the onslaught, he could sense defeat was in the air. This was indeed a time to panic—but he did not. While acknowledging the situation, he told them "The present situation is to be regarded as one of opportunity for us and not of disaster". The enemy armies had given them an opportunity by coming out of their defenses. Now, he expected them to take advantage of it. That general was Dwight D. Eisenhower. His leadership helped the Allies regain the offensive and helped seal the defeat of the German Army.

Years ago, I visited the Air and Space Museum in Washington, D.C. At the museum, there was an exhibit of air combat in Europe during World War II. At one of the displays, you can listen to the actual voices of a B-17 bomb-

---

1   https://www.nps.gov/eise/blogs/the-present-situation-is-to-be-re-garded-as-one-of-opportunity-for-us-and-not-of-disaster-dwight-eisen-hower-and-the-battle-of-the-bulge.htm

er crew as it was under attack by German fighters. When a crew member identified a German plane approaching, they would call it out over their intercom system. They would use a clock position, such as three o'clock (to the right) or six o'clock (behind them), to indicate enemy fighter positions. The callout was to alert the rest of the crew where the enemy fighters were located.

The bomber is under attack from German fighters. One can hear the crew frantically calling out fighter positions (i.e., three o'clock, six o'clock). As this is happening, the captain's voice comes over the intercom. In a cool, levelheaded voice he tells the crew not to shout but to call the enemy fighters' locations out calmly.

This crew is at 18,000 feet over enemy territory, fighting for their lives. It could all end in a second. They are combating very skilled German fighter pilots. The crew is nervous, they know what can happen in this type of fight. They understand how precariously their lives hang in the balance. It's normal to be scared and nervous, yelling. It's normal to panic—but it doesn't help. In the midst of this, the captain's voice reminds his crew to remain calm and gave them confidence and hope for survival. Now, if that captain could stay that cool while under attack during aerial combat, so can you and I.

When a crisis comes your way as it inevitably will—the next one is already on its way—the situation calls for a calm, level headed leader who can inspire others and help fix the problem. That leader is you. Even if you feel afraid or overwhelmed, staying calm is imperative. Panic is contagious; if you let it overtake you, it will in turn overtake your employees. Even if you are not 100 percent sure about what to do, project confidence. Take a deep breath and think through your options with a determined focus. This may take time to learn, and that's okay. Controlling your emotions from panic to calm takes practice. Make no mistake: reacting calmly to a situation doesn't mean you aren't engaged. You are fully engaged with what's going on around you. But learn to respond with a calm and controlled sense of urgency instead of panic.

There were many times in my career when I had to stay calm in the face of panic. One of these times involved a complainant to our agency, known as Mr. X. We had recently completed an investigation of a complaint requested by him that determined he would not be reinstated to his trucking job. Not surprisingly, Mr. X was livid. He began calling our office and harassing employees about our decision. It was light at first, but the more he called, the more his harassment became nefarious in nature. Employees eventually stopped taking his calls due to his abuse. Then he began using an alias to sneak around this buffer before launching into a curse-laden tirade. If you've ever worked in government, you know calls like this can happen, but they should not continue to happen. Mr. X never crossed a line until he left our office a voicemail saying he was going to blow our !@*# regulations right out the !@*# window. This veiled threat left employees feeling anxious. My employees thought that he was the type of disgruntled worker that could show up to our office with a gun and do precisely what he said. Once employees shared their concerns with me; I knew I had to act. This could be a life-or-death situation.

But as I'm sure many of you know, the federal government doesn't react quickly to anything. It took months to get something done. In the meantime, our office had no building security other than one small lock on the door. I had to project calmness and confidence to my employees. I was fully aware that Mr. X could, in fact, be violent and show up at our office at any moment. At the same time, I weighed the fact that the door to our office was locked and most important, Mr. X didn't know if we had security or not. While I was concerned, I certainly didn't want my employees to live in fear every day of coming to work. So I acted confidently in the face of panic—without downplaying the seriousness of Mr. X and his threats against the office. I told my employees I elevated the situation to upper management and reassured them that the issue with Mr. X would be handled. We went back over security procedures for the office, and we reinforced all identified weaknesses. As a team, we faced the problem together, all supporting one another.

I acted calmly, coolly, and deliberately in handling the situation. And my employees took their cue from my actions. Our office continued to run as normal, and our work was accomplished even though the situation with Mr. X took time to resolve. Eventually, armed federal agents went to find Mr. X. His wife had no idea he was making such threats. She was understandably upset to find this out from federal agents at her doorstep. The agents made it quite simple for Mr. X: *Call again and go to jail or stop calling and stay a free man.* We never heard from him again.

In approaching how to act in this situation, I listened carefully to the concerns of my employees. I didn't diminish their fears or chalk them up to overreacting. I took the time to sit down with them and hear about their experiences with Mr. X. I understood the gravity of the situation at hand. I then analyzed the situation and took appropriate precautions. I did everything in my power to keep fear from becoming panic. Most important, I projected calm to the office. I was nervous about what Mr. X might do, but I didn't show it. I continually reassured my employees that I and those above me were aware of the problem and were actively working to resolve it.

Panic is a natural response when we are confronted with fear and anxiety. Everyone experiences it to some degree in a leadership position. The panic may be related to less-dangerous causes, such as losing a big client or making a huge mistake that will affect the organization. Panic is natural, but your response to it is not. Learn how to deal with those feelings of panic and translate them into positive actions. Learn how to neutralize its grip and lead with your mind and rational thinking. I can always tell the leader in a room by who is panicking and who is not. That's where you want to be.

"How do you deal with panic when it comes your way?"

So, how do you do this? How do you deal with panic when it comes your way? Like the examples I provided, take a moment to analyze the situation. General Eisenhower met with his commanders to discuss the extent of the German army's penetration into American lines. They examined how big, how wide and how deep their lines had been broken. Then they talked about how they could turn a defeat into a victory. The pilots of the airliner that lost power kept communicating, troubleshooting, and helping one another. They worked as a team, never giving up even when it was clear the engines would not restart and they were going down. In my situation, I kept talking with my employees, analyzing the options, and planning how to disable the threat. In each of these situations, the call to panic was replaced by thoughtful, deliberate planning and response. Courage is found when you face a fearful situation and you defeat it.

I had a choice with Mr. X. To stay calm or panic. And sometimes, like me, you will have to remain calm for extended periods of time. Remember, your actions help others choose calm over panic. Your employees are watching you, and your choice on how to respond in difficult situations will also be their choice. Approach problems calmly and make thoughtful deliberate decisions. If you do, your free-falling plane will right itself, you will regain control, and you—and your team—will be flying once more.

This chapter on panic may have elevated your heart rate, so I want you to calm down, take a deep breath, and relax. And the next chapter is going to help you do just that.

Chapter 6
Lessons in Crisis Leadership
Key Takeaways and Applied Knowledge

Take it Further: Reflect on the key takeaways from this chapter and jot down your thoughts. How will you respond differently when addressing your next work crisis?

Chapter 7

QUIET NOW!

Lessons in Active Listening

You've probably heard this so many times before that you don't even think you need to read this chapter. I get it. You've been told to do this since you were a kid. Listen to your parents! Listen to your teachers! Listen to your coach, your grandmother, your spouse, [insert family member/friend/mentor here], and on and on. You've heard this all your life, and yet here I am again telling you to—listen. But don't tune me out. Listen (no pun intended) because doing this is essential to good leadership.

If you're going to make good decisions as a leader, ones that will benefit you, your organization, and your team, you need to be fully informed. You need to know what's going on around you. Listening to others is essential to this process. You need to build within yourself a listening mode where you filter for information. Listening is the process of gaining insight and intelligence. Listening will help you learn about updates on projects or tasks your employees are working on. It will help you make smart, informed decisions. You'll learn about employees' problems with an assignment or coworker that you need to address. And you'll gain critical insight into matters you need to know.

George Patton was a general in the U.S. Army who led American troops in Europe during World War II. He was one of the most successful American generals of the war. General Patton demanded up-to-date information be given to him twice a day—once in the morning and once in the afternoon.[1] All units on all fronts were required to report. He received reports from ground units, air units, and intelligence units. He even was briefed on summaries of daily newscasts. He was briefed on what was in front of his army and what was on its flanks. He was provided information from British, Canadian, and French allies. The entire briefing lasted about twenty minutes, twice each day.

After the general was briefed, the information was then shared with all the units of his army. So all parts of his army received the same information daily. General Patton listened to this wealth of daily information. Not only did he listen, but he also based his decisions on the information he gleaned during these briefings. He did this each day so he knew what was going on with the enemy in front of him. It helped him plan his next attack and upcoming strategies. He always kept his enemies guessing as to his next moves.

Whether you're a general fighting a major conflict with thousands of lives at stake or a supervisor over a few employees, it is critical that you take time to *listen*. If

---

1   Brenton Green Wallace, Patton and His Third Army, 2017, chap. 3, Kindle

you want to be successful, set aside some time to listen to your employees and customers. This isn't a task you make time for every once in a while or on special occasions. It's something you should do routinely. And frankly, every great leader has the time to do this. Can you imagine how busy a general of an army is during wartime? Yet General Patton took time each day, twice a day, to listen for information he did not know. You don't have to spend every minute of your day in listen mode or work overtime to do it. But if you commit time out of your schedule every day to listen, you will find a wealth of information essential to your success as a leader.

"Whether you're a general fighting a major conflict with thousands of lives at stake or a supervisor over a few employees, it is critical that you take time to listen."

In my job as a division administrator, I was responsible for the border operations of our agency in California. After a few months in my job, I became aware that there was grumbling going on among some of the border inspectors. I had to figure out what was going on. So, I decided to visit these inspectors without their immediate supervisor present. If they were having issues with their supervisor, I wanted to hear it from them directly. I informed the inspectors I'd be joining them as they conducted a bus inspection, and we could discuss what they were unhappy about. The day arrived, and I eagerly joined the inspectors for what I hoped would be a fruitful discussion. Instead, they were tight-lipped. The first fifteen minutes went by, and we had barely spoken ten words to each other. Their hesitation was palpable. Imagine you are in my shoes in this situation. What would you do? Walk out? Tell them you gave them a chance to speak and they blew it? I stayed and kept the small talk going. I was determined. I was there to listen, and I was not leaving. Something had to give.

About thirty minutes later, the inspectors began to open up and talk. And talk, and talk, and talk until they had opened up about everything that was bothering them. We talked for over an hour, and I began to understand the issue better. I learned how I could improve the situation. And I did. Had I walked out after fifteen minutes of small talk, I would not have understood what was going on. I would have missed the crucial information they provided. The problem would've become much worse.

Instead, I invested the time to listen. And the employees responded positively. They trusted me more after this meeting and they appreciated that I took the time to listen to them. Sometimes employees need time to feel more comfortable talking freely with their supervisor. I gave them that time, and so should you. Give them this time, and listen when they are ready to speak.

The best thing about becoming a better listener is that it's easy to do. Learn how to be quiet and listen to others. This works with employees, customers, or family members. The same principles apply. So how do you listen to an employee? What are the keys to making this work? Here are a few steps that will help you listen to your employees more effectively.

> *"The best thing about becoming a better listener is that it's easy to do. Learn how to be quiet and listen to others."*

First, be available to listen. Carve out time in your busy schedule to talk with your employees. Listen carefully to what they have to say. I've always had an open-door policy at my office. That means my door is open throughout the workday, and employees can come in and talk to me. Now, I already know what some of you are thinking. How is it possible to get any work done with people constantly coming in to talk at all times of the day? This is the biggest fear leaders have with such a policy. But it rarely happens like that. What will happen instead is that employees will feel comfortable stopping in and talking once in a while to discuss what's on their minds. If you happen to be busy when they stop by you can fix that by scheduling a time later in the day when you are available. I used this policy throughout my career and found it beneficial to obtaining good information.

Whether adopting an open-door policy or scheduling time, commit to listening to your employees. This is an investment in your success. It will directly impact your bottom line. This is not a waste of time. Take time to listen and make time to talk with them. This communicates to your employees that their feedback and concerns are important to you. They are worthy of your time and attention. Remember, when you listen to others, you obtain information that directly affects your job. As the leader in my office, I want to know when an employee experiences problems. I want to know if an assignment is going bad. I want to know if something happened in the workplace that I should be aware of. Like General Patton, I want to know what's in front of us, who's on our side, and where to go next. I need the intelligence. Making my team feel welcome to share information helps me do just that. It helps me address concerns before things get out of hand. I've avoided major problems simply by listening to my team and taking action based on what they told me.

Second, hear your employees out and don't interrupt them, even if you disagree. Of course, this is much easier said than done. Employees have told me that they felt their performance goals were too high. I sat there listening to them and disagreeing completely! It's easy to get defensive in such situations and immediately dismiss their concerns. It's easy to go into attack mode. You don't want to do that as it will only harm the relationship and result in less feedback. Instead, let your employee explain why they feel the way they do without interrupting or dismissing them. Ask clarifying questions to ensure you understand what they're telling you. Let them finish before you respond.

So when an employee told me their performance goals were out of reach, I asked clarifying questions about how long it takes them to complete specific tasks. Suddenly, the real culprit revealed itself. This employee let trucking companies string him along with requests to delay their inspections. I counseled the employee about our policy on this and how to respond when companies begin playing the delay game. I restated where our goals come from and why they are important. I reiterated my confidence that he could meet the goals we set for him. And guess what? He did meet them. After the meeting, there were no bitter feelings because I didn't attack him. I did not dismiss his concerns. I let him speak; I listened without interrupting. I then calmly discussed the issue with him.

Just because you take the time to listen to your employees doesn't mean that they will get what they want. It doesn't mean you will lower standards in response to their concerns. It means that you will hear them out and listen to their concerns. You will discuss the situation or problem they are facing. Employees appreciate you when you do this. Think about it—when was the last time your boss gave you their full attention to really listen to a problem you were having? When was the last time they asked clarifying questions regarding the issue and made you feel seen and heard? It matters to all of us. If you take the time to listen to your employees, they will talk with you. They will bring you information because they know you care.

Third, don't hold a grudge. Avoid reacting negatively when an employee tells you something you don't want to hear. One of the best things I learned to do as a supervisor was not to take offense when someone told me something I didn't like. Employees are not always going to inform you of things that make you happy. Nonetheless, you don't want to be running around all day mad at them because they told you something you needed to hear. They told you in the first place because they trusted you. This is the life of a leader. I get informed of things frequently that don't make me shout for joy. It goes with the territory. Deal with it. But I'm always better off knowing it than not. It's better to see the light and get a little annoyed than walk in darkness. Like General Patton, I'd rather know what's ahead of me than stumble into it—and get ambushed.

Some years back, there was a leader at my agency who was known for reacting negatively. When employees brought him information he didn't want to hear, he got angry. Just the mention of something unfavorable would upset him. His actions fostered an unwelcoming, negative environment. I remember attending a leadership meeting in Washington, D.C., where this leader was present. He gave the opening address, smiling and acting like a warm and welcoming person. At the end of his talk, he asked for questions or comments. I'll never forget it—there was not a sound in the room. Not one hand went up. Crickets! He asked again, and still no response. Getting kinda awkward. Then a third time and still complete and utter silence from the group. Finally, someone asked him a question, likely to save him from total embarrassment. This leader had reacted so negatively to feedback that nobody trusted him. Let this be a lesson for you: if your employees won't talk to you, it is because they don't trust you. And usually, this is a result of striking back at them when they attempt to share unfavorable information with you.

Finally, act on what you learn. Listening only works if you take action when a problem or issue is brought to your attention. When employees tell me they are running low on supplies to do their job, I submit a supply order immediately. If someone in the office is telling foul jokes, I step in and end the practice immediately. If I'm informed that we are citing companies incorrectly on our investigations, I get it fixed. Resolving problems as soon as possible is crucial to maintaining a high-functioning team. Employees quickly lose respect for you as a leader if you do nothing.

Recently my wife was having an issue with staff at a medical office. They continually informed her that they passed along the doctor's recommendation to another office. The other office never received it. This back and forth continued with no resolution. My wife finally called the office and asked the doctor to speak with her. The doctor did everything I covered in this chapter. She took the time to call my wife back. She listened without interrupting. She asked clarifying questions. She did not take offense. But best of all—she took action. Within a few hours, my wife received a call back from her staff. The problem was fixed. The office manager apologized and explained what had occurred. And my wife received her referral appointment and all was well. That sums up what listening is all about.

Listening is also important because it means you don't have to go it alone. Sometimes you should seek out others to listen to for wise advice. Before making a big decision, I always talk it over with those I trust. I listen carefully to their advice and input on the decision I'm facing. I ask them detailed questions so I can better understand the issue. This helps me select the best course of action.

The key to seeking wise advice is to seek it from someone you respect or admire. Sometimes I seek advice from those above me. Sometimes I seek it from my spouse and personal friends. Sometimes I seek it from my peers. Sometimes I seek it from my team if the decision will affect them. I might ask their opinion on a change in the office I'm considering. Somebody once said that wisdom is in the multitude of counselors. As a leader, gaining knowledge from others is essential. Seek it out from others when you feel you need to. It's good to hear

other perspectives. When you seek out advice, you will feel more confident in your decisions. And your choices will be better because you took the time to listen and gain input from others.

There is only one form of listening that I am not a fan of. It's something I encounter more and more today as a leader—the dreaded survey. You will hear that surveying your employees is the best method of gauging their happiness, thoughts, and comments. I disagree. Surveys are for those that won't take the time to listen to their employees. The federal government loves surveys, and they conduct one every year from their employees across the country. I did say every year, right? And whatever comes of this survey? Your guess is as good as mine. Most of the ones I've encountered in my work are so general that they are useless. If the supervisor would just take a few minutes each day to listen, employees will tell you all you want to know. I never had a survey come close to the knowledge and information I receive from directly talking with my team. And a survey will not fill this gap. Skip the survey and instead, take the time to talk to and listen to your employees.

Listening to others provides information that you and I need to be better leaders. I know all our lives we've been told to listen—and for good reason. It's essential you learn how to be a good listener. Good leaders are good listeners. Take the time to start listening better in all aspects of your work. Build this quality into your leadership style. The information you need to do your job better is waiting for you. You just have to listen for it. Start now. You won't regret it.

You are done listening for today, but the next stop in this book is where everything gets placed. It's the place where leadership begins and ends. It all stops here—with you.

Chapter 7
Lessons in Active Listening
Key Takeaways and Applied Knowledge

Take it Further: Identify one actionable step you can take immediately after reading this chapter to improve your listening skills.

Chapter 8

THE BUCK STOPS...

Lessons in Responsibility

This is it, the buck stops with... YOU. The last but by no means least aspect you must work on as a leader is to be the best you can be. You must fix yourself before you can fix anything else. So far, we've looked at several crucial elements you need to cultivate to become a great leader:

Look for your weaknesses—and fix them

Be honest and tell the truth

Be a hard worker

Don't run out of patience

Stay calm and avoid panicking

Make time to listen to others

If you spend time working on each of these aspects, you will be well on your way to becoming the leader you want to be. But there's one more thing we haven't covered yet, one more item to add to this list.

As a leader, you must take responsibility. All of the items we've covered so far involve responsibility in some way. When you're in charge, you must take responsibility for everything—what you say, how you act, how you work to improve yourself, what you know, how you exercise restraint, stay calm, how you listen, and how you achieve results. That's why the buck stops with YOU: No excuses, no explanations, no finger-pointing. If your ship is sinking, it's your job to save it. If people are not working or producing results as they should, your job is to get them moving. You cannot be a leader others look up to if you refuse to take full responsibility for your actions—and those of your team.

During my time as an investigator with the government, I often came across companies whose truck drivers were violating federal laws. When I asked company owners why nothing was being done to fix this, they would sometimes tell me, "Well, I can't make the drivers comply," or "They just won't do what I say." I didn't buy that excuse for a minute. These owners employ the drivers, pay them, assign them work, and now I'm supposed to believe the owners have no control over them. You have control over everything as a leader, whether you like it or not. Passing off blame to your employees as those trucking company owners did isn't going to fly. You are responsible for ensuring your employees are doing what they should, and if not, you are the one responsible for fixing it. Whatever the situation may be, you—and only you—are in charge.

There is nothing you can hide from as a leader. In my experience, I called the shots, hired and fired, assigned projects, reviewed work, drafted budgets, approved spending, and set goals. If something was done wrong, it ultimately fell on my shoulders. If we didn't meet our goals, that was on me. But that didn't keep me from losing sleep at night. Cultivating the leadership aspects we've discussed provides you with a strong foundation upon which to succeed. You won't be afraid to accept responsibility—you'll embrace it. You will learn that it is a natural part of being a great leader. It comes with the territory. And the mark of a great leader is someone who takes responsibility. And whether you accept it or not, it all falls on you.

I don't have complete control, you might be thinking. *How can I possibly be responsible for everything?* In my career with the federal government, there were many things out of my control. I had no say in the budget my office received each year. I couldn't decide on the salaries for the positions in my office. I didn't determine salary increases. I did not have complete control of hiring or firing, although I did both. I could go on here about all the things I did not fully control. Despite all of the things I couldn't control, what matters is that I took responsibility for those things I *did* control. And there were many! It's easy to become discouraged, focusing on everything you cannot change. Shift your focus instead to what you can control—and take leadership of that.

"I don't have complete control, you might be thinking. How can I possibly be responsible for everything?"

As a division administrator, I was occasionally asked to adjudicate employee discipline issues that occurred in another office. Our system was set up so that a supervisor who charged an employee with wrongdoing wasn't allowed to make the final decision regarding the matter. Instead, the final decision was made by another supervisor who had not been involved with the issue at all. One such employee discipline case was sent to me for review and final decision. A supervisor from another division was being charged with lying to his superior and faced a potential penalty of a five-day suspension without pay. Of course, the supervisor vehemently denied the allegation.

I read through the case documents and spoke with the employee who was accused of lying. Since he was a supervisor in the department, I held him to a higher standard of conduct than a regular employee with less responsibility. Yet I was shocked by what he told me. He refused to take even the slightest responsibility for his actions. He blamed his boss, his colleagues, the circumstances, everything. His excuses made him look small and unworthy of the responsibility that naturally comes with being a supervisor. So I upheld the five-day suspension. I only wish I could have spoken with him afterward to tell him how important it was that he change his conduct. Great leaders take responsibility for their actions and don't seek to blame others. I would have had more sympathy for the guy had he just owned up to the facts.

Taking responsibility is easy when you achieve success and those above you heap on the praise. It's not so easy when there is a mistake or a failure. I took responsibility when I succeeded and when I failed. I never blamed others, circumstances, or those below me. It was on me either way. I learned from my failures and eventually turned them into successes. That's a leader. Don't be afraid of this, but take it as a challenge to be the best you can be leading employees to achieve great things. Work on improving your leadership skills. They will provide you with a firm foundation for success.

But before you move ahead, make sure to give yourself time to practice the leadership qualities we've covered thus far. I cannot stress enough how important it is to work on yourself and your leadership abilities first and then focus on leading others. You must be ready to lead before you can lead others to greatness. Take your time on this—practice is a process. Go back and review these principles. And the truth is, you must continually review, practice, and work on these throughout your career. Nobody ever arrives at perfection in leadership. Every day is new and each one will have unique challenges. Each one of us must continually work at becoming better than who we were yesterday. And if you do, you will see the payoff in everything you undertake to accomplish.

Once you've gone back and reviewed the prior chapters and have started putting the principles into practice—and you're ready to take responsibility—then it's time to turn the page. Because in the next chapter, it's time to get off the bench and get on the court. The game is about to start. And yes, they are keeping score.

Chapter 8
Lessons in Responsibility
Key Takeaways and Applied Knowledge

Take it Further: Take a break to visualize how your life might change by applying the chapter's lessons. How could you become a better leader as a result?

Chapter 9

THE R-WORD

Lessons in Achieving Results

You'll hear this word all the time as a leader. It will become your main focus and goal, and it should occupy your thoughts daily. This word is why you're paid to lead others. It represents the difference you make as a leader to your organization. If you don't live up to this word, you will undoubtedly fail at supervision. What is this word I'm talking about? It's a simple thing called results. A leader makes all the difference when it comes to results. If you are not making a difference in your organization by achieving positive results, then you are, quite frankly, unnecessary.

Every single person in a leadership position must produce results for their organization. A general in the army must win battles in combat. A coach must win football games. A marketing supervisor must increase sales. A CEO must achieve good quarterly results. Everyone in leadership shares this same responsibility. And someone is watching for those results. Someone in your business is adding the numbers. Someone is keeping a score of how you are doing on results. And everyone faces the same fate if they don't achieve them. Whatever you want to call it—demoted, relieved of command, benched, or fired—you are no longer necessary to your organization. Keep your eye on results; that's why you've been chosen to be the leader. Be a results-focused leader.

Every leader needs to figure out the fundamental question: what is expected of someone in my position? What does success look like? What are those above expecting from me? Look at other successful people in similar jobs in your organization. What makes them successful? What is it that they accomplish that gets them promoted and honored? If you can't identify what success in your job looks like, then use the opposite. What does failure look like? One way or the other, you should be able to figure it out, and the sooner, the better. It's essential to know the correct answer because success is what you will strive to achieve as a leader in your organization.

Let's start with a simple example. A college basketball coach has many duties. She is an ambassador for the school she represents. She is a teacher and usually a mentor to the athletes. She attends fundraisers for the school's athletic programs. She attends high school games to scout young athletes to recruit. She has many duties, but one thing she better do above all is win games. All the other activities are needed, and they are important, but they won't on their own keep her employed. Winning games is what success looks like in her job. That's the ultimate result she's looking to achieve. All the other duties, without winning basketball games, are not success. She knows that going into her career—it's not a secret. That's the life of a college basketball coach.

Like a college basketball coach, you also need to be focused on answering this question because producing results, or winning games, whatever you want to call it, is your job. That's the job of every leader. Achieving results every week, month and year can be daunting. Ask any leader, and they will tell you that the pressure for positive outcomes can be overwhelming at times. It's not always easy to know where to start when you find yourself tasked with achieving results for your organization. So take a deep breath, and follow along as I show you how you can identify what success looks like in your work and how to go about achieving it. This chapter will help you create a game plan for success. Let's get started.

> *"I woke up one day, looked in the mirror, and did not like what I saw. I do this every day, like most people, but on this day, I did not like what I was seeing. I don't know why it took me so long to notice it..."*

Some years ago, I woke up one day, looked in the mirror, and did not like what I saw. I do this every day, like most people, but on this day, I did not like what I was seeing. I don't know why it took me so long to notice it. I probably saw it earlier but ignored it. But on that day, I could not ignore it. I looked overweight. Not really, really, overweight, but not where I should have been. A quick check of the scale showed me that I was correct in my assumption. I was about fifteen pounds over where I belonged. I was determined to change it. What weight did success look like for me? Around 175 pounds. That was my goal. How do I get there? I had to do something different because I would not make my goal if nothing changed. I had to change something to lose the weight.

I knew that I could not lose weight overnight. I'd seen people make that mistake too many times trying to lose it all at once only to gain all the weight right back. But I wanted to reach my goal. I had to set some stepping stones in place to achieve success. I needed new activities that would help me reach my goal. To do this, I reduced my intake of carbohydrates, watched my portions at mealtime, and incorporated aerobics into my workout routine. The result? Well, it took time; remember the chapter on patience? But I lost the weight. I got down to 175 pounds and have maintained it for over twenty-five years. That's success. And this same process works in business.

Set goals that lead you to success. Let's say success is getting to the top of a steep hill. But you can't get there in one step; it's just too steep to climb. This is where you would set up stepping stones to help you get to the top. Each stone could be used for footing, and each one would help you reach the next one. Eventually, you would work your way to the top of the hill. Let's go back to the basketball coach example. Success is winning games, but how does one get there? Winning games is not easy. The basketball coach knows that she must apply some short-term and long-term stepping stones to achieve success. In the short term, she increases aerobic training and improves her players' core skills. In the long term, she commits to expanding the sources for recruiting new players. The coach uses short-term and long-term stepping stones to bring her team success. You and I need to do the same.

In 1961, then President of the United States John F. Kennedy issued a challenge to the nation. He wanted to land a person on the moon within ten years. That may not sound that extraordinary to us today, but it was a big deal back then. You see, in 1961, the U.S. had no way of going to the moon. The U.S. space program was in its infancy, and it could barely circle the earth. The vehicles and propulsion systems needed to go to the moon had not been developed. The computers, software, and guidance systems that would be required did not exist. All these things were yet to be realized. And yet, the president challenged the nation to land a person on the moon within ten years.

The National Aeronautics and Space Administration (NASA) was tasked with accomplishing the president's vision. They began to tackle the big challenge with a series of stepping stones. They started developing and testing new technology. They sent astronauts into space to test new propulsion and flight control systems. Each mission got them closer to their goal of going to the moon. In 1968, NASA sent Apollo 8 to circle the moon a few times and then return to earth. Finally, on July 20, 1969, Apollo 11 landed a spacecraft, and a person, on the moon. It was a crowning achievement of nearly ten years of work. And it was not possible without many intermediate stepping stones that helped NASA overcome every obstacle on its way to history.

As a supervisor in my agency, one area of responsibility was overseeing the agency's safety grant program. A grant is a contract that provides money to a state or organization to perform specific work for the federal government. The state of Illinois conducted work for my office under one of these grants. My office monitored their work for quality, quantity, and timeliness. As we monitored the state's progress on this grant, I realized there were substantial issues with the quality of work they produced for us. In the beginning, the quality was, well, let's say it was less than optimal. For example, shoddy report writing, incorrect citations being written in response to violations, and inaccurate numerical data were found in their reports. Success in this program required a significant improvement in the quality of their work, and it was my job to ensure the state took things up a notch. It was time to set some stepping stones in place.

In the short term, I increased communication with the state partners and focused on the quality issue within their reports. When issues were found, my office clearly explained what was wrong, why it was essential to be correct, and how they could improve. I made our office staff available for their employees to call directly with questions, and I met more frequently with them to review specific quality issues. My staff conducted training classes for their employees to help them become more proficient. These things worked to an extent. Quality did improve. But I realized that to get to the level needed to achieve program success, the state needed to improve quality control on its end. I needed the state to dedicate the supervisory resources necessary to perform better quality control.

It took time to convince the state to commit to the plan and commit the necessary personnel. But it paid off, and the quality of their work improved substantially. This resulted in decreased workload for my office and better program results because of the improved work quality. My short-term stepping stones to address the quality issue were essential to start the improvement process. But it was the long-term stepping stones that made the significant program improvement that enabled lasting success in that program.

Keep in mind that stepping stones and goals to success can change over time. What leads you to success today probably needs adjusting to remain successful for tomorrow. I stated earlier in this chapter that I've maintained my initial weight loss for twenty-five years. How-

ever, the stepping stones I used to achieve my goals have changed over time. I had to incorporate new ones, such as reducing alcohol consumption and eating more fruits and vegetables. The same goes for leadership; you have to continually ask the question of what does success look like and how do I get there. The world is constantly changing, and to achieve long-term success, you must change with it.

Chapter 9
Lessons in Achieving Results
Key Takeaways and Applied Knowledge

Take it Further: Set a specific goal inspired by the chapter and outline a plan to achieve it.

Chapter 10

R'S FOR EVERYONE

Lessons in Managing for Results

As a leader, a big part of achieving results is leading employees. If employees don't produce good results, neither will you. There are some good rules to follow to ensure those under you are making the grade. And your goal should be to get the best from them, to bring out their potential, and let it rain results for you as their leader.

How does one do this? It starts with clear expectations. You can call these performance goals for each employee. Each person who works for you should know what is expected of them. Don't assume they know; make sure they know. There's nothing worse for morale than when employees are not aware of what is required of them. When employees don't know what you want, they will do whatever *they* want instead. And this will not get you the results you need to stay in a leadership role.

In the government, we were given our performance goals in writing every year. There was no excuse for saying, "I didn't know..." At a minimum, goals need to be personally communicated to each person. Each person should know their individual performance goals. Why is the employee there? What is expected of them? The leader sets these expectations and communicates them to their employees. Your team's success, and ultimately your success, depends on each employee working toward goals. Again, they don't need to be complex. Performance goals can be as simple as delivering excellent customer service, responding timely to emails, getting letters out on time, or increasing sales. As the leader, you set the expectations for what your employees will achieve. Your responsibility is to ensure that employees know what you expect of them.

In the government, I communicated expectations to my employees primarily in two ways: in writing at the beginning of the year and in staff meetings. I reminded them of what we were all there to do, what their job was, and what I expected of them. No secrets, no guessing, it was straight and to the point. This was done in a positive, uplifting manner. Employees catch on quickly when you communicate with them honestly. You can do this without being condescending, harsh, or making threats.

A leader's job is to communicate clear expectations so employees know what's expected of them. And my goal was for my employees to succeed. When they did well, so did I. When they hit it out of the park, so did I. I enjoyed seeing my employees flourish in their jobs. It was a sign that I was doing my job well.

When you set employee expectations, they need to be reasonable. If you set the bar too high, you risk discouraging your employees and hurting morale. On the other hand, if you set the bar too low, you will end up with mediocre performance. It's about finding the right balance. The goals you set should be challenging, but they shouldn't be impossible—employees will get bitter and start looking for other jobs. And you will find yourself in continual hiring mode, constantly training new folks who won't stay long due to the frustration of trying to meet unattainable goals. It isn't sustainable, and it isn't necessary. A boss of mine many years ago told me that he wanted me to give him an honest eight hours of work each day. "If you give me just eight good hours," he said, "everything will work." And he was right. I respected him for treating me as a person instead of a machine. It's essential to show the same respect to those you lead.

> *"When you set employee expectations, they need to be reasonable. If you set the bar too high, you risk discouraging your employees and hurting morale.*
> *On the other hand...*
> *if you set the bar too low, you will end up with mediocre performance."*

As you set expectations, be open to listening to employee concerns, even if you disagree (sound familiar: remember the Quiet Now chapter?). Calmly listen to what they say and reply with justifications about why you set that job expectation for them. You should articulate why the expectation is required and how it ties in with your organization's overall success. All the expectations you set should support one overarching goal. If they don't, what's the point? When I was questioned on my expectations for an employee, I would explain why they were needed and how they were related to the success of our office. I would restate that what I was asking from them was reasonable and that they could do it. In the end, if employees are unable or unwilling to meet your expectations, then they are in the wrong job. You can nicely convey that message, but when push comes to shove, that's the bottom line. It has to be this way in business. A leader is about achieving results. And you can't achieve good results when some employees can't or won't meet your reasonable expectations. It won't work.

Chapter 10
Lessons in Managing for Results
Key Takeaways and Applied Knowledge

Take it Further: Create a checklist of action steps inspired by the chapter. Do all your employees have clearly communicated goals?

Chapter 11

EYES ON THE GAUGES

Lessons in Monitoring for Results

I was piloting a small airplane approaching the airport at Myrtle Beach, South Carolina, when it hit me. I was flying through clouds in moderate turbulence. I was in training to learn how to fly an airplane without visual reference to the ground. I had a hat on which did not permit me to see outside the windows. I could only fly using the airplane's flight gauges. Things were going well, and then it happened. It started slow but began to get stronger until I realized something was wrong. I was getting conflicting data that was downright dangerous. One piece of information was in my head, and the other was on the instrument panel. And they did not agree with one another.

In my head, I began to feel a sensation of a slow turn to the left that kept going until the plane became inverted. This is not a good thing to do when in the clouds and at a low altitude. Suddenly I felt like I was flying upside down. I was terrified. But, the flight gauges on the instrument panel showed the airplane level and flying straight. I had a flight instructor in the co-pilot seat next to me and he was not screaming or trying to take the controls. That also did not make sense. I fought hard to focus as I could not understand what was happening. The tendency in this situation is to follow your feelings and turn the flight yoke to reverse the airplane's perceived inverted attitude. But that would be a fatal error. Because the plane was just fine, I was the one who had the problem. I had just experienced spatial disorientation and survived it for one reason.[1] I chose to fly by the flight instruments, not by how I felt. After about 30 seconds, all was good again. It was a good lesson to learn as a pilot. It's an even better lesson to learn as a leader.

Think of where you are today and what success looks like for you. Think about the short- and long-term stepping stones you need to put in place to guide you to the results you desire. They don't have to be complex; I recommend keeping them simple. Write them down and look at them; remind yourself where you plan to go. This is your blueprint for success. This is how you produce great results. This is what being a leader is all about. But hold on, just a few more moments. Because just having well-placed stepping stones and clear expectations is not enough. It's a good start, but there is something else you must add. And it's just as important as the stone itself.

"Think of where you are today and what success looks like for you. Think about the short- and long-term stepping stones you need to put in place to guide you to the results you desire."

---

[1]   A condition that creates sensory conflicts and optical illusions that often make it difficult for a pilot to tell which way is up. (FAA Pilot Safety Brochure AFS–850 16–05)

How do you know the plans you put in motion are working? Are you relying on your feelings for how things are going? How do you know employees are indeed meeting your expectations? How do you know they will produce the results you are looking for? I'm glad you asked. There is a way to know the answers to these questions. I call them gauges and they are an invaluable management tool.

If I were riding in a car with you and asked, "How fast are you going?" What is the first thing you would do? Would you try to calculate the speed in your head? Would you guess how fast you were going? No, probably not. You would look at the speedometer, the gauge that displays vehicle speed. Do the same thing with stepping stones; put a monitoring gauge on them—preferably a gauge that contains a number. You set up the gauge, and then you check it periodically. The gauge will let you know if you will get to your goal or miss it entirely. It will tell you how fast you are going or if you are standing still. Looking at the gauge, you will know precisely how far you are from realizing the goal.

Gauges are the way you measure progress on a goal or a stepping stone. It's something that summarizes data and provides you with an easy-to-understand result. They become your eyes and ears on how you are doing. They are instruments that, once connected to data, will provide you with critical information. A gauge can be

a spreadsheet, it can be a report, or it can be a piece of paper with summarized data on it. Its purpose is to remove the subjective feeling of how you are doing towards reaching a goal and make it more scientific. And based on the type of goal, you may need more than one. Again, think of your car; it has several gauges like fuel and temperature. They work to ensure you get to where you want to go. And they give you peace of mind along the way as you glance at them that all is good.

But the gauge is not just for enjoyment and feeling good; it can be a signal to take action. When my car's fuel is getting low, I start thinking about refueling. The gauge communicates that I don't have many miles left unless I want to push the vehicle myself. Therefore it spurs me into action to avoid an unpleasant outcome. And that is precisely what they will do in your professional life. They will give you confidence that you are on track or spur you into action to make adjustments. Either way, they lead you to success. And you should set them in every area of your responsibility.

My work with the government required me to deliver results in many areas. One of those was conducting a certain number of investigations on trucking companies. My office was expected to produce high-quantity, good-quality, and timely investigative reports. Every day, I made it my goal to ensure that my office and employees remained focused on achieving the goals set by my agency. I knew that success centered around achieving results in this area.

How did I know my office was on track to meet goals? How did I know my stepping stones were working? I took measurements and set gauges, of course. I kept detailed spreadsheets that summarized vital data points for my office and each employee. I ran the numbers for each person and each office I led every month. I calculated where we should be for that time frame and where we were actually at. I did this every month for years during my career. It was no doubt the best thing I ever did. Each month I knew exactly where we were in relation to our set goals. No guessing. I knew if we were on track to meet the objectives or not. And if not, then I needed to adjust something to get back on track. That's why you set gauges and take measurements. You don't wait until the end of the year to find out you've gone off the rails. You set gauges, monitor frequently, adjust if necessary, and keep meeting your goals.

You also need gauges for your employees. Set up a monitoring system to periodically check how each employee is doing. Maybe once a month, once every other week, whatever works for you. Keep the gauges focused on their work's quality, quantity and timeliness. The gauges will tell you which employees are doing well and which ones are not. Look for trends and take appropriate action when you notice a negative pattern. Taking action is crucial to stop downward trends from continuing—and getting worse. And don't forget that someone else is looking at the same data. Don't be in a position where it has to be brought to your attention for action. You should know about the problem before others see it. That's the purpose of monitoring.

As you set gauges, be careful not to beat your employees over the head with them. I didn't hound my employees 24-7 about their numbers. If you have kids, you know that nagging them 24-7 makes them bitter. Nobody wants bitter kids. You also don't want resentful employees. And nagging your employees will make them bitter, resulting in many other adverse effects. There's a better way.

> *"As you set gauges, be careful not to beat your employees over the head with them."*

It's an art to decide when to get involved and how to get an employee back on track. Sometimes it requires encouragement, and other times, it takes a more forceful hand. I recommend using the least-aggressive approach first. If I could get an employee back on track without formal discipline, that was a win. But if not, as a leader, I had to get results. And sometimes, that meant getting tough.

Achieving results is one of the hallmarks of outstanding leadership. It represents the difference you make as a leader in your organization. Remember, identify success, place stepping stones towards your goal and set gauges to monitor progress. And these three items, identify, place, and gauge, are continuous. They repeat over and over again - creating a pattern for successful results. You never stop doing them. It enables you to lead your team to bigger and better accomplishments. And when all is said and done, that's the job of the leader. You're there to get results. You are there to make a difference. You are there to make things better. A great leader gets results. Remember the R-word, results, and always make it a part of your daily routine.

Chapter 11
Lessons in Monitoring for Results
Key Takeaways and Applied Knowledge

Take it Further: Challenge yourself to re-examine the gauges you have to monitor success. Are they working? Are they useful? Could new ones help you improve your results?

Chapter 12

TOUGH LOVE

Lessons in Corrective Feedback

An associate finds her manager in a public place at work and asks why she isn't getting challenging work assignments like her peers. "I received complaints about your work from a few individuals, so you'll need to improve to get those assignments," the manager tells her. "When did you receive complaints about me?" the associate asks. "Oh, a few months ago," the manager responds. The associate then asks who complained about her work, to which the manager replies by naming a few of her coworkers. "Why was I not informed of these complaints?" the associate asks, bewildered. Her subsequent questions seeking specifics about the allegations are rebuffed.

To get the information she wants, the associate then confronts her coworkers alleged to have complained about her. And she discovered that each person mentioned by the manager denied that they had made a complaint. Instead, they told her the allegations were false and that the manager was not being truthful.

Do you find anything troubling about this story? It was an actual event, and it's a perfect example of how not to give corrective feedback to an employee. First, a leader never gives corrective feedback in public. Employees deserve privacy when their job performance is being discussed. Even when an employee starts a conversation in public, as the associate did, it is the supervisor's responsibility to move that conversation to a private room or office where no one else can overhear the situation.

Second, feedback was not provided to the associate in a timely manner. The manager allegedly received complaints months before but never told the associate about it until now. If feedback is essential, it must be given promptly. It isn't fair to the employee or others involved when months go by and no action is taken.

Third, the allegation is too vague for the employee to know exactly what they need to improve. Corrective feedback must be as specific as possible to make it clear to the employee what isn't working and how they can fix it. When a supervisor is vague about an employee's performance, they are either not telling the truth or exaggerating the issue.

The time comes when every leader has the unenviable task of giving corrective feedback to an employee. So what exactly is corrective feedback? It's feedback given to an employee when they have done something wrong or didn't perform as expected. Maybe someone sent an inappropriate email to others. Or maybe a tasteless joke was shared in the break room. Perhaps an employee isn't performing up to your set work standards or goals. Whatever the case, there's an effective way to handle it. And it must be addressed, or you will likely get the same behavior or performance repeated.

The goal of giving corrective feedback is not to destroy the employee, crush their morale, or ruin their career. On the contrary, the goal is to set them back on course, set clear expectations for them, and change their behavior. Many supervisors don't like to do this, and I get it. It isn't pleasant to tell someone they've messed up. You never know how the employee is going to take it. But it's essential to the success of your team. You can't ignore bad behavior or poor employee performance—it negatively affects everyone's morale and ultimately will hurt your efforts to achieve results. It must be directly addressed as soon as possible. As with many other responsibilities and tasks, giving corrective feedback is an essential skill of a good leader.

For example, an employee's reports are consistently late, and it's having a negative impact on your team. How do you effectively address this problem? The first step to providing corrective feedback is to call the employee into your office to discuss the issue privately. And before you ask, no, an email doesn't count! Sending an email is fine for letting an employee know you want to meet with them to discuss their monthly production numbers or whatever the topic might be. But it is a sign of a true leader to provide corrective feedback in person, face-to-face. This conveys the seriousness of the issue to the employee. You can directly engage with them and observe how they respond. There are times when you need to handle matters in person, and this is one of them. If you cannot meet with the employee face-to-face—maybe they work remotely or are traveling due to the nature of their work—the next best option is to provide corrective feedback over the phone or by video conference. This will still convey the seriousness of the issue better than an email ever will.

Once you've scheduled the meeting, make sure you stick to the issue at hand. When the employee comes into your office or calls you, get right to the point. Small talk about the weather or weekend plans trivializes the tone of the meeting and makes the employee believe they aren't in that much trouble. Instead, state the problem as directly as possible: I called you in today because the last four reports you turned in were late. Be specific. Which reports are you talking about? When were they due? When were they turned in? It's imperative that you provide such information in as neutral a manner as possible. This isn't a time to accuse or embarrass the employee, but rather to review their behavior or work performance and explain why it needs to change. Remind the employee of the conduct and work performance standards you expect them to meet. "You know our reports are due within five days of completion," I might say to an employee. "I expect you to meet that timeline." Or, "telling coarse jokes in an email to the office is inappropriate and will not be tolerated." Clarify your expectations so the employee knows what they need to do to meet them in the future.

After explaining the issue at hand, it's time to give the employee a chance to talk. It usually takes them a few moments to fully comprehend everything you've just said. And it can get quite awkward when they don't immediately speak—but wait for it. You are waiting to make sure the employee understands why their behavior is a problem. You also want to make sure that your facts are correct. Sometimes the employee has more information to share that better explains their actions. It's happened to me before in corrective feedback meetings. What you are hoping for by listening to the employee is that they will acknowledge the problem, take responsibility for it, and provide assurances that it will not happen again.

At this point, you'll get one of a few possible responses from the employee. A good employee will readily take responsibility for their actions, apologize if necessary, and fix the issue. During the COVID-19 pandemic, a few of my employees struggled to adapt to the new normal of working off-site. They struggled to meet their monthly investigation numbers while working remotely. It was a difficult time for everyone in the agency, and I tried to be as accommodating as possible. But at the end of the day, we still had goals to meet. We still had results we needed to achieve. So I directed my supervisory employees to call each person who was behind on their production numbers and give them the corrective feedback talk. And one of those employees, when confronted about her low productivity, took responsibility and asked for help. I can't tell you how much I appreciate it when someone responds like that. She didn't deny the facts or make excuses but asked for help meeting her productivity goals. That's what the corrective feedback talk is ultimately about—fixing issues, keeping good employees, and improving results.

Unfortunately, not every employee reacts so graciously. You're more likely to deal with an employee that begins to throw out excuses for their actions. "It isn't my fault because of [insert excuse here]." "I intended to turn my report in on time, but [insert excuse here]." Believe me, you will hear every excuse in the book. It is your job to make such an employee take responsibility. Restate the standards of performance you expect. Tell them you expect them, like every other employee, to meet that standard. Make it clear that you will not accept excuses, especially when other employees meet the expectation without difficulty.

You might also get an employee who deflects responsibility. When confronted about their actions, they will change the topic or blame someone else entirely. Maybe they'll now want to tell you secrets about another employee who is doing something wrong too. If they start deflecting, you must immediately refocus them on the issue at hand—their behavior! Employees deflect because they don't want to face the consequences of their actions. It's easier for them to talk about other employees than it is for them to defend their performance. Instead, firmly keep the issue on the employee and hold them accountable for their behavior.

Contrary to popular belief, giving corrective feedback to employees doesn't have to be confrontational. You don't have to raise your voice, get angry and curse to make your point. And in fact, you shouldn't. Remaining calm, cool, and collected will convey corrective feedback far better than angry outbursts ever will. Remember, you're looking to solve the problem you're having with an employee, not make it worse.

I once gave corrective feedback to an employee who suddenly broke down crying in the middle of our meeting. Trying to compose herself, she told me she had just broken up with her significant other and had to move out of their apartment. I felt awful, and I hated making her feel worse. As leaders, there is so much that goes on in the personal lives of our employees that we will never know. Handing her some tissues, I gave her a few minutes to regain her composure before gently continuing our conversation about her work performance. As much as you hate piling on to your employee's bad day, there's no getting around the problem. If you wait for the perfect moment to provide corrective feedback to an employee, you'll wait forever. So, as calmly as possible, I reminded her of the performance goals I expected from her and explained that I was there to help her achieve them.

Treat your employees with the utmost respect, even when they are failing at something. They're only human. And most of the time, they already know they are coming up short. They are their own worst critics. Providing corrective feedback respectfully and calmly reminds your employees that you're an ally there to help them rather than an enemy out to destroy them.

After your corrective feedback conversation, there's just one last thing you need to do: Write down what happened. Summarize what you discussed with the employee, how they responded, what questions they had, etc. Make sure to include as many details as possible. The point of taking notes about the meeting is to document your attempts to correct a problem with an employee. If the employee's performance doesn't improve after the corrective feedback meeting, you can pull your notes out and review what you discussed with them. If you reach the point of terminating the employee, your notes act as evidence justifying your decision. Date the notes and store them in your files, not the personnel files HR keeps for each employee, but your personal files. Taking notes of corrective feedback meetings is one of the most important things you can do as a supervisor. On more than one occasion, my notes reminded me of exactly what I said to the employee during a previous meeting. And this helped me remember their prior statements and their promises to improve.

Providing corrective feedback to employees is never fun, but it is essential. As the leader, it is your responsibility to hold employees accountable for their actions and job performance. It is your job to get employees back on track when they stray from what they're supposed to be doing. An organization cannot be successful, healthy, and results-driven without leaders providing corrective feedback when necessary. Believe it or not, corrective feedback—when given appropriately—increases morale. Employees who work hard and achieve great results want to see those who don't held accountable. They also want to see that bad behavior is dealt with swiftly.

Over my career, I've had these challenging discussions with outstanding employees, as well as those who were not so great. And looking back, I'm proud of how many of these employees went on to become valued workers. Many went on to get promoted. My talk with them did not crush them, it did not ruin their career, it helped them succeed. I helped them repair an issue they had, and in the long run, it benefited everyone. I still take pride in that accomplishment. And that's what corrective feedback is all about—achieving success. It's not always pleasant, and not all respond positively. But it's something that a leader must do. And if you do this right, you are helping yourself and your organization succeed.

Don't avoid corrective feedback. It will enable you to cultivate improvements and better performance from your employees. And that's the goal. Remember to do it face-to-face, promptly, privately, and give the employee specifics on the issue. Then listen, and follow through with what you feel is needed to address the matter.

But as with everything else in life, nothing is guaranteed, not even corrective feedback. There will be times when it fails, and you'll be left with just one option.

Chapter 12
Lessons in Corrective Feedback
Key Takeaways and Applied Knowledge

Take it Further: Identify a corrective feedback conversation with an employee that you've had. How would you have done it differently after reading this chapter? What lessons can you apply to future conversations?

Chapter 13

END OF THE LINE

Lessons in Removing Employees

If you thought giving corrective feedback was uncomfortable, wait until we get through this chapter. When corrective feedback doesn't work and the employee refuses to improve, you've reached an impasse and it's time to part ways with them. Firing someone is never a pleasant task, and even after years of serving in leadership positions, it never gets easier. Letting an employee go can be a tough decision to make. It's sad to remove an employee from your organization permanently. It's frustrating that they didn't work out as you had hoped. Despite all of the corrective feedback you provided and the assistance you offered, in the end, sometimes an employee cannot or will not change for the better. For the sake of your organization, you need to find someone who will do the job correctly. So how do you manage this in the best way possible?

Every organization has different rules for how and when to fire an employee. The federal government has an extensive process for removing employees. It begins with numerous meetings with human resources about the employee's poor work performance and a review of documentation. If the effort to remove is approved, the employee still gets one last chance to improve their performance over a 30-60 day period. The employee is given a step-by-step guide on how to meet the standards of the job and what is considered passing or failing. And the employee can challenge each step of this process, filing grievances to human resources and making the entire process way more complex and confrontational than it needs to be.

Even when the agency finally does remove them, the employee has the right to file an appeal with the Merit Systems Protection Board. That board can overturn the removal if they determine it was unjustified or proper procedures were not followed. The supervisor removing the employee can be called on by the board to provide testimony regarding the removal in a court-like hearing. Your firing process may be easier or more difficult than this (although that's unlikely). Either way, I'd like to give you some pointers that will help you when you face the unpleasant task of letting an employee go.

First, work closely with your organization's human resource (HR) office. My HR department was invaluable to me when I had to fire an employee. They helped me understand the process, fill out paperwork, and ensure my documentation was adequate in case of appeal. When an employee files a grievance against their termination, the HR folks will usually help you respond. They will do everything they can to save you from going to court over a termination lawsuit. And even if you do have to go, they will help you win.

Another benefit of consulting HR is that you want them on your side. It was so much easier to take action against an employee in the federal government once I had HR on my side supporting me. Most of the time, HR has more experience than you dealing with these messy issues of firing employees, and their job is to protect you and the organization. Consult their advice as soon as you think you may be heading down the path of firing an employee.

Now, consulting HR doesn't mean they will always agree with the action you want to take. Sometimes HR will give you advice that you don't want to hear. They may ask you to provide more evidence to justify firing an employee. They might even tell you that you don't have a strong enough case for termination. If you disagree with their decision, be sure to ask for clarification. Make your case as to why the termination is warranted. On a few occasions in my career, it was my push that caused HR to change its opinion and support firing an employee. In one case, I had to show HR why termination was the only option. In cases like this, it is absolutely critical to have documentation to support what you're trying to do.

This brings me to the second step of dismissing an employee: Evidence. Remember the importance of taking notes after corrective feedback meetings? Those notes become crucial evidence once you start the process of firing an employee. To prove why firing an employee is justified, you need to show documentation of what they did wrong, what performance standards they failed to meet, and how you tried to help them. Providing such evidence protects you and your organization from litigation.

Don't underestimate how jilted employees can react to being fired. They can sue you, drag you before bureaucratic state boards, and generally cause you much grief. Be prepared for it. As the old saying goes, prepare for the worst, but hope for the best. Gather all of your evidence together and hope that you won't need to use it.

What types of evidence am I talking about? Personal notes regarding corrective feedback. Copies of emails to the affected individual and their replies. Notes and emails from other employees tasked to work with that individual—statements the person made, copies of deficient work items. Statements customers made about the individual. Data reports that show performance relative to other employees. I've had to produce each of these elements at one time or another in my career. You need evidence when you are the official that is terminating an employee. The evidence protects you, and it protects your organization. Even if you own your own business, you should keep this evidence in your records. You'll be glad you did this the first time someone challenges a termination.

I also recommend that you build a case for removal with more than one failure occurrence. For example, if an employee failed to meet their prescribed goals for three months in a row, this would be adequate cause to begin the termination process. I know it takes more time to do it this way. And I also realize that for some failures, such as driving impaired in a company vehicle, the firing may be immediate. But generally, the more you can show a pattern of behavior or non-performance, with the appropriate critical feedback given in response, the better off you are. By doing this, you provide the employee with more opportunities to demonstrate that they can meet your organization's work standards. And you provide yourself with more evidence to sustain a removal and improve your chances for success in case of a challenge.

Documenting an employee's performance also helped me fire employees without feeling like a total jerk about it. I never enjoy firing someone—it's an unpleasant task. It's especially unpleasant when the employee begins crying, telling you sad stories and how desperately they need the job and the money. Or that if you fire them, they will lose the only healthcare they have. Those are real-life situations that I've dealt with. Yet, in each case, I warned the employee about their performance on numerous occasions prior to the actual dismissal.

There was considerable documentation of poor performance or improper conduct. The employees were notified and spoken to about it, but to no avail. They were given ample time to change and improve, yet they didn't.

At some point, patience runs out. Bad behavior or poor performance continues, and the decision to terminate the employee is made. So when the tears and sad stories came, I didn't waver in my decision. No matter how compelling their situation may be, no matter how I may feel personally about the employee, I cannot make decisions based on my emotions. Notes and documentation of bad behavior and work performance helped me justify my decision legally. And just as important, it helped me maintain my humanity throughout the grueling process.

The last step in firing an employee is to let them go with dignity. Don't fire employees in public. I've heard stories of supervisors asking employees to leave and carry their personal belongings out in view of the whole office. All this does is further hurt and embarrass the employee on an already bad day. It is never acceptable to hurt someone for no reason. So if you decide to fire someone for valid reasons, that's fine, but do it in the right way. Have the conversation in a private place where no one else can listen in. Treat the employee with as much respect as you show to everyone else in the office. They deserve no less respect because they are being terminated.

I remember on one occasion when after I had fired an employee, she told me she needed time to regain her composure. She asked me if she could leave the office and return after hours to gather her things from her desk. Now,

I just told you earlier to consult HR, right? If I had called HR to ask them if I could allow this employee to come back after hours, they would have said no in a heartbeat. You may disagree with my decision here, but I felt it was the least I could do for this employee. I agreed and arranged for another supervisor to let her in after hours and help her move her stuff to her vehicle. She had thirty days to file an appeal challenging the legality of her termination. But she never filed. Oh, my office would have won the case, I'm sure (I keep meticulous documentation!). But I like to believe she never filed because I treated her with dignity during the firing process. I accommodated her request to gather her belongings privately and wished her the best in the future.

When someone is fired—even when it is absolutely justified—they have suffered a great loss. They have no job, no power, and are facing an uncertain future. Don't add to the burdens a terminated employee is already experiencing. You would want the same if it were you.

> *When someone is fired—even when it is absolutely justified—they have suffered a great loss.*

One last thing is how to tell the rest of your team that someone was let go. This can be tricky depending on where you work. I was not at liberty to disclose personnel information on an employee in the federal government.

But I felt it was important to get ahead of the rumor mill, so I informed everyone that so-and-so was no longer with the organization. I left it at that. If asked, I would say it's not something I can discuss. They would eventually figure it out. But not from me. Also, don't run people down after they're gone. It makes you look small to do so. Show respect to the departed employee, no matter how incompetent they were. You still have others looking at you—the current employees. Don't rejoice, don't sing a happy song. Just go on about the business. Set the standard of respect no matter what the situation. It will help you keep your sanity and show others what an effective leader they have.

> *"I informed everyone that so-and-so was no longer with the organization. I left it at that. If asked, I would say it's not something I can discuss."*

Firing brings one issue to an end. But get ready because there is another situation heading your way—and you didn't see this one coming.

Chapter 13
Lessons in Removing Employees
Key Takeaways and Applied Knowledge

Take it Further: Consider how the chapter relates to current events in your workplace. Are there employees nearing the end of the line in your organization? What actions should you be taking right now?

Chapter 14

———

SMALL EXPLOSIONS

Lessons in Incident Response

Have you ever watched a slow-motion video of a bomb exploding? It's truly amazing how something in such a small package can ignite and cause incredible destruction. How is it that something that appears so small has the potential to release enormous energy and cause a massive reaction? The same thing happens in organizations all the time. Minor incidents among employees can blow up and cause huge problems. As a leader, it's crucial to know how to respond when this happens to you.

Let's start with an example. An employee comes to your office and says another employee bumped into them without apologizing. It sounds like a minor, inconsequential event, right? No big deal. Maybe tell the parties to go talk it out? Well, something similar to this happened to me which resulted in a complaint filed with the Equal Employment Opportunity Commission (EEOC), hours of legal depositions (legal jargon for being questioned by attorneys under oath), and a trial. Not so small, after all.

Here's another one: Several employees are eating lunch in the break room together. As one of them goes to sit down at the table, she suddenly falls to the ground. She claims another employee moved her chair, causing her to fall and hurt herself. Again, this sounds like a minor thing, right? The employee who fell is likely more embarrassed than physically hurt. Yet this, too, resulted in an EEOC complaint, a claim filed for disability allegedly caused by the incident, and countless hours of legal responses and meetings.

These examples illustrate how seemingly minor incidents can cause big problems. But there are two significant differences in these examples: In one of them, the office supervisor took the correct action to address the situation, while in the other, no action was taken. And the incident in which the supervisor took action was ruled in favor of the organization. The other was never fully settled.

So what action should you take when confronted with such incidents that would seem to be so inconsequential and minor? In many cases, they seem so trivial that the supervisor does not bother to address them or investigate them properly. You need to view these types of incidents as a fuse that has been lit. If that lit fuse hits the dynamite, something that seemed so trivial can blow up on you. And it isn't pleasant when it happens. I've had to deal with what I call small explosions numerous times throughout my career. By following some basic procedures, you can significantly increase your chances of successfully defusing these situations.

The first step to addressing a situation is to act quickly. If two employees get into an argument and one claims the other pushed him, it is your responsibility to hear him out. The employee is telling you about the incident because he feels he was wronged. It may or may not have happened exactly as described to you, but the employee believes that it did—and that's all that should matter to you as the leader. *Come on, Steve*, you might be thinking, *this is minor stuff! Everyone's an adult here; there's no need to take it so seriously.* While it might be tempting to brush such problems off as a waste of time or an employee being melodramatic, these minor incidents can explode into huge lawsuits if you aren't careful. A minor incident initially reported to me as a bump or a push later changed to assault and battery. Trust me, the smallest, most innocuous incidents between employees can blow up into massive, messy legal battles that you'd much rather avoid at all costs.

Now, I don't want to give the impression that you need to perform a full, months-long investigation for every single incident that occurs in your organization. For example, if two employees get into a verbal argument and say some mean things to each other, I'm not going to open an investigation. I would quickly counsel them and move on. Serious incidents—ones that involve physical contact, harm due to negligence, or the use of demeaning language—always require a response. But before you can determine the best course of action to respond, you need all of the facts of what happened. Facts are easy when everyone admits to what they did. But that does not always happen. You will undoubtedly run into occasions where the employee who allegedly committed wrongdoing denies anything and everything about it.

> *"The first step to addressing a situation is to act quickly. If two employees get into an argument and one claims the other pushed him, it is your responsibility to hear him out. The employee is telling you about the incident because he feels he was wronged. It may or may not have happened exactly as described to you, but the employee believes that it did—and that's all that should matter to you as the leader."*

Remember—these are not criminal acts I'm talking about. If someone is punched in the face and beaten up in the office, that is a criminal act. You need to call the police. The incidents I'm talking about here are not violent acts but could involve unwanted contact, like a bump in the hallway. For example, they could involve a female employee receiving unwanted attention from a male employee. The person accused isn't a criminal but still needs to be questioned about what happened. It's essential to keep an open mind during this process. You may think highly of one of the employees involved in an incident. They may be a great worker who has never caused an issue before. Even so, follow the facts where they lead and reach a fair and unbiased conclusion. If you feel you can't be impartial in your investigation, have another supervisor conduct it.

After an incident has been brought to your attention, it is crucial to immediately talk with each employee involved. Not only will memories still be fresh in their minds, but you'll be able to take note of their initial statements before they have time to change them. A bump today might become a push tomorrow after they have more time to think about it. I had this exact scenario happen to me. Good thing I had the foresight to take statements from the employees involved the day the incident occurred. It was apparent who was changing their story to make it appear worse. And it didn't work because of my diligence in getting the information right after it occurred.

Don't just talk with the employees involved; speak with those who may have witnessed the event. Again, get them to commit their recollection of events as soon as possible. I would speak with those involved first, then potential witnesses. I would write notes, entering the time and date as I questioned them. And then, I would ask them to send me an email again re-stating what happened. In this way, I confirmed their account of the incident in person and in writing.

When you question employees, begin by asking open-ended questions. Let them talk. For example, "Tell me what happened," or "Tell me what you witnessed."

Then listen (remember the chapter on listening - Quiet Now!), and ask follow-up questions to fill in the gaps. By starting with open-ended questioning, you will get more details of what happened. Start with the person making the allegation. After they tell you what happened, you can ask more specific questions to fill in the gaps. Press for details as they are critical. You need to fully understand the allegations and everything that occurred. Take notes as each employee recounts the incident and compare them afterward. If you've got two different stories of what happened, you know someone isn't telling the truth. And what I've found over my thirty-year career is that the one telling the truth will maintain a consistent story of events no matter how many times you ask them to recount it. The one not telling the truth will change their story over and over again.

I had an employee who had an incident with another employee, and as he was telling me about the incident, he brought up another issue from the past. He stated that he had previously been told a racial joke by this same employee. The past incident had nothing to do with the current one. However, since he brought it up, I had to address it. After he told me the "what happened," I asked him what the joke was. He seemed caught off-guard by my question. Maybe he thought I would not ask that. I did not ask the question because I wanted to hear the joke. I did not want to listen to the joke. But I had to document the alleged "joke" because that's an important detail. Had the accused employee told the joke before?

To my amazement, the employee could not remember the joke. This goes to the question of who is telling the truth. This was not evidence that his current incident was untrue. But it did bring into question his credibility. Had I not pressed him for the details, he would have gotten away with it. One does not complain about a bad joke that when pressed, one can't remember. The employee was blowing smoke on this one. When we concluded, I asked him to think about it and return when he remembered the joke. He never did. But when I interviewed the other employee, I did relate the allegation and asked him directly about it. These are not comfortable situations to find yourself in. But they happen, and as a leader, you must address them by asking good probing questions to get to the truth.

Once you speak with each employee involved in an incident and take detailed notes of what they tell you, it's time to review the information to determine if you have all the facts. In one case, I discovered additional witnesses to an employee altercation whom I hadn't yet spoken with to get their take on what happened. So I made arrangements to interview them as soon as I could. I also went to the location where the incident was alleged to have occurred to see if everything made sense. I visited the office where two employees bumped into each other. Was the room laid out as they told me it was? Is it plausible that two employees could bump into each other in this space? These are the kinds of questions that can shed a lot of light on the situation at hand.

Visiting the site of the alleged incident, I found that the employee making the complaint misstated how the office was laid out. That's a big mistake. His story said that he had to walk around a chair in the office, which brought him closer to the alleged bumper, but the office had no such object in it. These little details are incredibly important because the other employee—the alleged bumper— described the office layout exactly.

Investigating such details may not be necessary when there are many witnesses to the incident or if one person admits to causing it. But in some cases, both employees vehemently deny the other's story. In those cases, every bit of information matters. I'll say it again because this is very important: The person telling the truth will have a consistent story. The person who is lying will continually make changes to what transpired. Looking for discrepancies in their stories and investigating the location where the incident occurred will help you determine what actually happened.

OK, so you've done all of the above steps. You took initial statements from the employees involved in the situation, you took detailed notes, and you had them submit emails to you. You interviewed other witnesses and took notes from them, too. You went to the location to veri-fy the stories. Now what? Now, you need to make a final written record of what you did, what you discovered, and what you concluded. Don't panic; this doesn't need to be a book. It's just a detailed recollection of what you did and what you found. Such a record helps you remember exactly what happened and will help you if the employee incident ends up in court. It may go nowhere but always be prepared for the worst.

Be factual, to the point, and only draw conclusions based on the evidence you've found. Avoid using phras-es such as "I don't think the employee was telling me the truth," but rather "The employee's statements contradict-ed those of numerous witnesses." See the difference? One is based on conjecture, the other on evidence. Stick to the facts and conclude what you found. If you can't draw any final conclusions from the evidence, be honest about that.

My written records of employee incidents have been used in court to clear employees and our agency of wrongdoing. In one particular situation, my report was re-quested for review over and over again. Your notes as the supervisor have weight, and when you follow this process to record the truth of a matter, it can have a significant impact. Some incidents you'll face will take on a life of their own and last for years. And usually, they are minor incidents that you didn't see coming. Having a report on the incident and the steps you took to resolve it not only protects you and your employer but also ensures that you don't forget any key details about what happened.

Minor incidents among employees can quickly blow up into bigger ones and cause huge problems for you. As a supervisor, it is essential to act quickly to get to the truth. Your efforts to defuse the situation can save you and your organization lots of time and money. Now that you know how to respond, you will be able to handle them appropriately and effectively. And hopefully, your efforts can prevent a minor incident from blowing up into something much bigger.

Now that you can withstand small explosions, there is another type of issue you need to be on the lookout for. This one is not clear-cut, but the stakes are even higher.

Chapter 14
Lessons in Incident Response
Key Takeaways and Applied Knowledge

Take it Further: Discuss the chapter with a colleague or counsel and get their perspective. Do you know the procedures to follow in your organization should incidents occur?

Chapter 15

GET YOUR EARS UP

Lessons in Workplace Protection

One of the most challenging things you may encounter as a supervisor is an employee that could become a security risk. Maybe they are acting strange. Perhaps they said some disturbing things. Perhaps they don't talk at all but just have a constant scowl on their face. Or maybe you just sense that something isn't right. What do you do?

A crucial aspect of being a leader is protecting your employees. You must constantly be on the lookout for signs of a possible employee problem that could spiral out of control and put others in danger. You could be the person that defuses a dangerous situation in your office. You may be the one who prevents a tragedy from occurring. Your actions could mean the difference between life and death.

Sadly, workplace tragedies are far too common. We've all heard news reports of a disgruntled employee going to work and shooting fellow coworkers. In many cases, there was no clear sign they had such violent intentions. It's impossible to know exactly what's going on in employees' lives or predict how they will act. But as the saying goes, hindsight is always twenty-twenty. More often than not, red flags about an employee's behavior present themselves before such tragedies occur. And it's your job to be on the lookout for them.

According to the Bureau of Labor Statistics, in 2018, 453 workers were victims of workplace homicide. Most of the victims were male. However, just as disturbing was the fact that in 2019, 20,870 workers experienced trauma from nonfatal workplace violence. Of these, sixty-eight percent were female, and seventy percent happened to healthcare and social assistance workers. This is an issue that impacts you as a leader because it's your job to protect your employees. And while this chapter will focus on internal threats, you also need to be mindful of external threats to your employees.

To be clear, this chapter focuses on employees who you suspect may be a danger to themselves or others. The keyword here is "may." You don't know for sure. They may not have threatened or harmed anyone. They may not have made any death threats or posted anything concerning on social media. But, for some reason, you still have a nagging uneasiness about them. You might have noticed a significant change in their behavior—for the worse. Maybe the employee is a loner and doesn't associate well with other employees. Perhaps they become irritable quickly at the slightest inconvenience. Whatever it might be, something about this employee makes you wary.

But being wary about an employee is not a justification to fire them. You can't just dismiss an employee over unproven concerns. You cannot remove union workers over conduct they haven't committed. From a legal perspective, it's almost impossible to fire an employee without due cause. Now, if the employee makes a direct threat, whether on social media or to another employee, that's a different story. Immediate termination of employment in a situation where direct threats have been made is entirely justifiable. In fact, it's absolutely necessary.

Employees should feel safe at work and not be subjected to threats made by a coworker. Cultivating a safe work environment is essential to retaining and recruiting high-quality team members. Don't take the risk of retaining a troubled employee that may bring harm to your team. Instead, remove employees who make threats against others. This in itself can be dangerous since the fired employee may try to take revenge for their termination. But it's much safer to deal with them outside of your organization rather than from within.

One of my managers once felt uneasy about an employee she supervised. She always sensed something could be wrong with this employee, even though the employee in question had never made any threats or harmed anyone in the office. Yet it was clear to the manager that the employee was mentally unstable. Even so, the employee did their job and continued meeting performance goals. Yet the uneasiness persisted.

Have you ever seen a rabbit or deer in the wild? When they sense something is close to them, their ears perk up. They stop what they're doing, stand as still as a statue, and listen to the environment around them for any threats. You need to do the same. When you sense that gut feeling that something isn't right with an employee, you need to watch them more closely. Listen to what really might be going on, and be on guard against any threats. That's what the manager of this employee did. She was constantly on the lookout.

Eventually, the manager started noticing disturbing trends. The employee started becoming more irritable in the office. Interactions with other coworkers became toxic. The employee's attitude and demeanor became negative. And it wasn't getting better with time. When news reports of mass shootings occur, there are usually clues in the perpetrator's actions leading up to the tragedy. The manager feared such changes in conduct were indicative of something more serious, so she shared her concerns with human resources.

The manager could not have been more correct. Sometime later, the employee began seeking a medical determination to essentially retire from their position. This process involves a personal evaluation of an employee's mental or physical fitness for their job.

It was during the evaluation with a counselor that the employee began railing against her supervisor. She made a statement to the effect that if she had a gun, she would shoot her supervisor. The counselor immediately communicated the threat to our agency, and the employee was swiftly removed from service.

Thankfully, everything in this case worked as it's supposed to. The manager sensed a problem, was on guard and made sure others were aware of her concern. She consulted with human resources, followed their advice, and continued to monitor the situation. The FAA counselor didn't hesitate when she heard a threat from the employee and reported it quickly. Everyone took proper action. And as a result, nobody was hurt. Just as animals in the wild switch into high alert mode when threats lurk nearby, you need to stay on your toes and on the lookout for potential threats in your workplace. How you handle such situations could mean the difference between life and death.

Each potential threat you may face in the workplace will be different. While the details of these situations change, one thing will always stay the same: Your responsibility as the leader is to safeguard your employees. It's your job to notice and be on alert for any dangers. And most importantly, it's your job to act when a threat has been made.

In another situation, an employee in a field office started to exhibit several behavioral concerns. The person was isolated, angry and not getting along well with other employees. He exhibited a short fuse and would blow up in rage over the most minor inconveniences. These changes were sudden and surprising. Usually, this employee was known to be a good worker. He took his job seriously and produced excellent work. But over time, his direct supervisor started noticing a decline in productivity, along with the concerning behavioral changes. So what did she do? You guessed it. She kicked into high-alert mode. The manager came to me to discuss her concerns about this employee. She covered every detail of what was going on, why she was concerned, and what potential steps we could take to prevent a bad situation from becoming worse. After our conversation, she remained on the lookout and took a step I hadn't anticipated.

During the manager's subsequent discussion with the employee, she found an opening to talk to him about his recent conduct in the office—the negative attitude and unruly temper. During that conversation, the employee opened up to the manager and explained the personal challenges he was facing. His honesty was a key factor in resolving how she could assist this struggling employee. The manager offered to help the employee through the agency's various mental health programs. We don't know if he took her advice and sought out assistance. But we do know that his behavior changed for the better. He still had some issues, but the manager did not think he was contemplating violence. And he never made any threats.

My manager deserves all the credit. She knew he was struggling, made her concerns known to me, and took action to solve the problem. And it worked. She was not afraid to talk with the individual to gather information. She confronted him, in a constructive way, about his behavior and offered him help. This is exactly what you want to do in similar situations: get the employee to talk to you. Look into their eyes and see if you pick up anything. Listen for anything that appears to be a threat against you or another employee. Get them talking, and then see what your next steps should be. The employee I referenced earlier—the one who threatened to shoot her supervisor—only conveyed the threat when talking with a counselor. Talk to other employees and see if they heard anything that could be perceived as a threat. Get your ears up—and listen to what the employee is communicating to you or others.

It goes without saying that you should always ask for guidance when confronting these situations. Ask for help. Meet with human resources, legal advisers, and counselors if you have them available. None of this is a guarantee that you will be able to prevent workplace violence. But—and this is crucial—you have to do everything in your power to try. As the leader, you have to make an effort to promote safety and well-being in your organization. You can't ignore it. Your job is to keep everyone safe. Do something. It's always better than doing nothing.

Behavioral issues and the potential security risks they pose are never easy issues to handle. If you are in a situation like this right now, I encourage you to stay on the lookout for any threats, consult with others in your organization about your concerns, and bulk up security if need be. Remember, the vast majority of employees don't hurt others and won't go on shooting sprees. But it's always a good idea to be on the lookout for signs that a situation may be deteriorating into something dangerous. Take reasonable precautions necessary to ensure tragedy doesn't occur in your workplace.

"Behavioral issues and the potential security risks they pose are never easy issues to handle."

The final aspect of being on the lookout involves your employees. Ask them to report concerns they may have, and work with them to help make the workplace a safe and free from harm zone. Encourage them to speak out when they see something troubling and report any social media posts by employees that could suggest potential workplace violence. Train all members of your team—supervisors, managers, and employees—to be on the lookout for concerning behaviors and communicate that with management. Most of all, keep talking to the employee you're concerned about. Keeping an open line of communication with them, as the manager in my office did, lets them know they are a valued member of your team and that help is available. Following these key guidelines means you'll have multiple lines of defense in your workplace that make it harder for an employee contemplating violence to keep it a secret.

More helpful information on this topic is available from the U.S. Bureau of Labor and the National Institute for Occupational Safety and Health.

Chapter 15
Lessons in Workplace Protection
Key Takeaways and Applied Knowledge

Take it Further: Explore additional recommended resources for deeper learning.

Chapter 16

THE RIGHT TOUCH

Lessons in Delegation

I'll never forget one of the first do-it-yourself plumbing jobs I did in my first house. It seemed easy enough to fix the water pipes leading into the tub spout. I went to the store and purchased the replacement parts. I read up on the repair; it seemed pretty straightforward. I told myself that I didn't need to pay those high fees for a plumber. This repair would be easy. And thankfully, it was easy. I made the repair, and it worked—for a while. But later in the week, to my horror, I noticed a spot on the kitchen ceiling. *Oh, what could that be?* I thought to myself. Well, it didn't take me long to figure it out. I knew what it was. It was a water spot. Not good.

Plumbing is one of the most frustrating home repairs I have attempted. I've had some bad experiences, like the one I just described. And I've had other occasions when things did not go quite like I planned when fixing a plumbing issue. The worst part is when the entire family looks at you like, "you don't know what you are doing." I got better at it and have some good success stories also. But plumbing also taught me something about leadership and control. In plumbing, the way you do something matters. When you tighten a fixture, there is a way to do it that works and a way that does not work. Too tight, and it will leak. Too loose, and it will leak. Just the right snugness, and it works. The same goes for how you lead employees. If you are always on them, too-tight micromanaging, it will produce negative results. You will cause your employees to stagnate. Micromanaging only increases resentment between you and your employee and is an inefficient use of your time. You will be running around with little time for your job because you are always doing everyone else's job.

On the other side, if you are too loose with your over-sight of employees, it can also produce subpar results. You need just the right touch to lead and guide them to successful results. It's more of a skill than a science. And often, like plumbing, if your approach is failing, you may have to loosen a bit or tighten a bit. But always lean toward growing employees, and don't tighten unless you have to. Because like in plumbing, over-tightening not only causes leaks but it can also ruin the fixture you are working on.

A friend of mine related a story about a boss he had who was a true micromanager. This boss was constantly on him about every little aspect of his work. If that isn't frustrating enough, one time, this boss sent a memo (we didn't have email back then—I know that's difficult for some of you to grasp!) about how my friend was parking the company car wrong. This wasn't just a regular memo explaining which spot to park in or when to take the car in for routine maintenance. No, it was a full-page memo specifying to my friend exactly how much space there needed to be between the vehicle and white lines of the parking spot, how much clearance room to have to the front and rear of the parked car, and exactly which light he needed to park under for security.

My friend, who had to put up with this type of management for far too long, decided to write his own memo in response. First, he thanked the boss for his detailed instructions on parking the company car. Then he reaffirmed each instruction to make sure he understood exactly what he was being asked to do. And then my friend pointed out to his boss that, although the memo he sent was good, he left one crucial question unanswered. He ended his response memo with that one question: Shall I pull the car forward or back it into the parking spot?

Nobody likes a micromanager. You know the kind. In fact, you've likely experienced this type of boss at some point in your career. A micromanager treats their employees like children and tells them exactly how to do every little detail of their jobs. They can't stand not knowing every single thing that's going on in the organization, so they dictate everything. It's a suffocating oversight. And it doesn't benefit anybody. Micromanagement demoralizes employees by telling them they can't be trusted to do the work they were hired to do. It breeds mediocrity, prevents growth, and stifles good employees. Talk about a morale killer.

"Nobody likes a micromanager.
You know the kind. In fact, you've likely
experienced this type of boss at some point
in your career."

Micromanagement doesn't harm only the employees subject to it. It negatively affects the micromanager, too. One thing I've noticed about leaders who micromanage is that they are constantly stressed out. They are simply doing too many jobs at once instead of the most important one—their own. As much as micromanagers may think their actions promote an efficient, hardworking office, they actually end up creating way more work for themselves. Employees quickly learn they can't make decisions without their boss's complete review and approval. So instead of working through simple problems or questions on their own or with the help of a coworker, employees go to their micromanager boss to decide how to handle every issue they encounter.

The micromanager ends up doing work employees can handle on their own. Their actions create less individual responsibility, more stress, and more work. This is all due to the boss refusing to cede even the tiniest bit of control to others. And worst of all, it makes employees feel small and not appreciated.

Remember the R-word we discussed in a previous chapter? Achieving results for your organization is crucial to effective leadership. Yet micromanaging employees will sink any hope you might have of leading your office to bigger and better things. Remember, you have the higher-level job that nobody else in your organization can do. Your focus needs to be on steering your ship toward results and ensuring everything runs smoothly in the process. Because if you're busy doing the work that your employees can and should be doing themselves, then who is steering the ship? Before you know it, you and the workers you lead will be sinking under the weight of unmet expectations and goals.

The opposite of micromanagement is delegation. It's learning to trust others to accomplish work for you so that you can focus your efforts on big-picture things. Now, I'm not saying you shouldn't know what is happening at the micro level of each employee's job. Let's use a ship again as an analogy to make this point. If I'm the captain of a ship, I'm cognizant of the electricians who keep the power running. I know what their responsibilities are, even if I'm not in the belly of the ship telling them exactly how to hook up the wires. Do I check on the electricians once in a while? Of course. Do I ask them questions about their work to know what they do every day on the ship? Absolutely. This allows me to have a basic understanding of the electrical process and how their work enables the ship as a whole to function like it's supposed to. But since the electricians are the experts, I give them the space they need to work efficiently. If I hovered over their shoulders each day telling them which wires to hook up and what to do next, I'd only create frustration among the electricians and leave the ship's wheel unattended. Instead, I trust them to accomplish this critical work while I focus on steering the ship.

If you are worried that employees won't complete tasks as well as you would or be as thorough, then equip and train them with the skills they need to succeed. Instruct them on how to produce the quality work the organization requires. Give them room to grow so they can learn from both experience and their mistakes to produce better results.

I always found it interesting when I attended national meetings and conferences where some of my colleagues were constantly on the phone with their employees back in the office. They were continuously shooting off emails and answering calls from their employees, who apparently had questions that couldn't wait until their boss returned. Thankfully, I've never had this problem. When I left the office, I gave my employees the responsibility to run the place in my absence and the authority to make decisions and handle issues that arose while I was gone. As a result, I rarely received urgent phone calls or dire emails from them asking me how to handle a problem. Not only did this relieve me of much stress, but it also helped my employees grow. They gained valuable experience leading an office and learned the art of good decision-making. And if employees are not maturing, that means you as a leader are failing. Because part of your job description is to make everyone you are responsible for develop and grow professionally. And as your employees gain knowledge and confidence, your job gets easier. And better results get produced.

That's the beauty of delegating work and not micromanaging your workers. Employees gain confidence in their abilities when you trust them enough to handle tasks and projects independently. They begin to take more leadership roles because your actions show them they are capable of it. As employees manage their responsibilities effectively, you can oversee the product of their work and ensure everyone is helping the team achieve the results you expect. And don't get me wrong. You still hold employees accountable if they aren't achieving the results you need them to. But you don't have to suffocate them with micromanagement for them to up their game.

> *"By giving your employees the space to handle responsibilities on their own, you are helping them cultivate their leadership skills. It's a win-win for everyone."*

Of course, just the opposite is true if you micromanage. When your employees know that you don't trust them to handle issues independently, you create dependents who cannot think or make decisions themselves. Instead, everything revolves around you and your decisions. In situations like this, employees do not have the opportunity to grow as leaders. Instead, their growth is stymied by constant micromanagement that tells them they are neither capable nor trusted workers. Such negativity only further reduces their job morale and, in the end, hurts the results you want your organization to achieve. And the person leading all of this is more stressed-out than ever as it becomes harder to manage. Micromanagement is a downward spiral that only damages an organization and its workers. But the good news is that it's never too late to change course.

***

Now, there will be times when you need to get in the weeds of your employees' work. But don't stay there long and get back to managing for results as soon as possible. I enjoy reading about great military leaders, and one of those great leaders was U.S. General George Patton. I briefly mentioned him in an earlier chapter of this book. He was the commanding general of the Third U.S. Army Division in Germany during WWII. His army of over one hundred thousand men was engaged in some of the most critical battles in World War II that helped decide the war's outcome. He had tremendous responsibilities as the leader of the Third Army. He was under immense pressure to attack and defeat the German army. As a general leading an army in combat, he had no time to waste. He constantly listened to intelligence reports to determine where the German army was located, what they were planning, and where he could best attack them. He had to lead his army into battle against a well-trained and capable opponent. He had to assess his numbers constantly, his men, tanks, artillery, and how to best use them for victory. He had to ensure he had sufficient supplies, ammunition and food to keep his army moving. He didn't have time to microman-age, but he occasionally did.

General Patton was known to direct traffic once in a while as his men and tanks advanced against the German army. An army has many vehicles during wartime such as tanks, troop carriers, supply trucks, jeeps and heavy guns. Soldiers who served under Patton during the war told stories about him directing traffic and urging them to keep after the enemy.[1] In the movie "Patton," played by George C. Scott in 1970, he is depicted as a hero and great war general and at times a traffic cop. In one scene depicted in the movie, he noticed a traffic jam was hold-ing up his tanks and men from moving forward. He could have had someone fix the problem as it was well below his rank to address. But he did not do that. He got out of his jeep, into the mud, and began directing traffic. He's yelling, waving his arms, and nobody dares not follow his directions. He got the traffic jam fixed and everyone mov-ing again. Directing traffic in a war zone when you are a general leading an entire army—that's micromanaging at

1   John Niesel, *Howitzers, Grasshoppers, and the Holy Right Hand*, 2008, p. 126

its best. But of course, the general did not always direct traffic; he could not do that and win the war. You get the point. Sometimes you may have to micromanage, but it should be the exception, not the norm.

Micromanagement is sometimes necessary even when not leading an army, such as when dealing with an immature employee. When an employee demonstrates that they are not responsible, trustworthy, or dependable, you may have to micromanage them to get them back on track, if possible. Notice I say "if possible." This type of behavior should ultimately result in termination if not corrected. Immature employees, unfortunately, need to be micromanaged because they are unable to manage them-selves. I once assigned work to such an employee task by task instead of giving him several assignments to work on over a few months like everyone else. I made him report his progress to me at the start and end of each week, while mature employees only had to report to me once a month. I made this employee put together a daily schedule of ac-tivities he planned to accomplish and detail exactly what work he did each day. It was a lot of work for him and me. Yet all these extra steps were necessary because this em-ployee was incompetent and was not getting the results required. In the end, the employee left my office and the agency. And we were both better off for it.

Be careful not to treat all employees the same, how-ever. Everyone is at different maturity levels. Just because

I had to deal with one immature employee in my office didn't result in treating everyone else in the same way. Mature employees who could successfully handle responsibilities on their own were given the leeway they needed to achieve results. Reward those good-producing employees by delegating tasks, giving them room, and helping them flourish. Don't restrict them with the limits you may have to put on others who are not yet mature enough without tight oversight. It was only the immature employees who had to be micromanaged. Don't punish everyone for the faults of a few, but instead manage employees to their level of maturity.

And remember, the goal is to develop and grow employees to excel in their jobs and become leaders. When employees grow professionally, so does the company they work for. When employees grow, so does the supervisor who leads them. When employees grow, so do the organization's results. When employees grow, so does morale, confidence, leadership, and I could go on here for a while. But you get the point. Make things grow.

So how do you do this? How do you figure out the "right touch" when leading employees? First, go back a few chapters and review "The R-Word" chapter. In there, I detail how you manage employees for results. Hopefully, you still remember the lessons of that chapter, but if not, stop here, and go back and review. How you manage employees (i.e., delegation versus micromanaging) is directly related to the results you produce. And that chapter shows you how you do this—remember to have goals, set expectations, and measure results. Go back over that chapter if you forgot because it's important. And it will help you to see how to delegate, lessening the need to micromanage.

You also have to train employees to see growth. There is nothing worse than bringing new employees into an organization and not providing them adequate training in their jobs. Because they haven't been adequately trained, they constantly require assistance. They don't know how to achieve what is expected of them. Invest the time to train your employees. I can tell right away when I visit a business or a fast-food restaurant whether the employee is trained. And the difference is significant; it's a big, big difference. Your customers notice this. Training or the lack thereof affects results. Employees who are trained can answer simple questions and solve simple problems without having to call the supervisor. They have some authority to help a customer. And there is something else I notice about these folks. They seem to be happier and more motivated. It's a beautiful thing to experience. Teach them how to do their job and give them some space to thrive. You'll be amazed at the results.

One of the ways my agency trained new hires was by assigning a coach or mentor, an experienced person who worked with the new trainee for a set time to help prepare them. We still had formal classes for the trainees, but the hands-on instruction with another skilled worker was very effective and proved an excellent training method. We typically kept the training intense for six months. During this time, the coach and the trainee performed the job together and worked the same schedules. And the new trainee learned from one of our best. After six months, the trainee began to work independently with occasional oversight from the coach. Eventually, the new employee was out on their own producing good results. It took time and it took resources, but it worked. Our folks were well-trained and that training subsequently paid off. In time, the trained person is asked to mentor a new employee, and the process begins again.

You don't have to have a six-month training program, yours could be six weeks, it depends on the job and the level of skill and knowledge required. Growing employees starts with the day they are hired, and you have to invest in it. The initial training gives them a solid foundation for building on in the future. And each time they grow, you and your organization win.

Finally, give them the opportunity for growth. When I was out of the office for any length of time, I left some-one in charge. It was not the same person each time. I would allow each one of my subordinate supervisors the opportunity to lead in my absence. I would email the other employees that this person was acting for me in my ab-sence. I did this so they could gain invaluable work experience and improve their problem-solving skills. And even though I checked my emails when out, I let them handle the ship. Only on rare occasions did I involve myself when I was out. They grew into better leaders as a result. And my organization benefited the most because I was developing potential leaders left and right. That's the job of a leader—to make things grow.

While micromanagement may be necessary for certain situations, it should be used sparingly. Otherwise, it destroys employee morale and turns what should be self-sufficient workers into inefficient dependents who require your approval to do anything. Manage employees for results and give them the opportunity to grow and become effective leaders themselves. You'll end up having more time for the job you were hired to do and lead your team to even better outcomes.

Now that you know how to manage employees in the right way, it's time to send them a message. But be careful because what you send is not always what others receive.

Chapter 16
Lessons in Delegation
Key Takeaways and Applied Knowledge

Take it Further: Take a moment to reflect on the chapter's message. What is your management style? How could you adjust your style to produce better results?

Chapter 17

I CAN'T HEAR YOU...

Lessons in Communication

I learned how to fly an airplane from an old instructor who taught me everything he knew from decades of flying. He once told my flight class about the number of general aviation crashes that occurred where the pilot never asked for help. Whether running low on fuel or encountering bad weather, he explained that some pilots simply kept on flying without radioing in for assistance. His lesson here was so simple, yet it ended up saving my life. When you are in trouble, you need to communicate—and clearly.

A few years after this lesson, I was spending as much time in the air as possible to fulfill the FAA's forty-hour in-flight time to be eligible to take my pilot test. As I flew high above eastern North Carolina destined for the Johnson County airport near Raleigh, the weather started to deteriorate. My visibility declined significantly so that all of a sudden, I could barely see the ground. At the time, I wasn't certified to fly in heavy clouds or fog. And since I couldn't see the ground well, I didn't know how to find the Johnson County airport, let alone land there safely. With half a tank of fuel left, I wasn't panicking. I had enough fuel to get home. But I was concerned. I reached the point where I decided it would be wise to seek some assistance.

I knew there was a military base nearby—Seymour Johnson—so I made a call for help. *Seymour Johnson, this is Cessna 68762.* No reply. I could hear voices on the channel, but they were busy tracking military aircraft. I called again. *Seymour Johnson, this is Cessna 68762.* Still nothing. Okay, now I was getting a little panicked. I looked at my fuel gauge diminishing and at the ground that I could barely see. I remembered all those stories my flight instructor told the class about pilots crashing without ever making a call for help. I heard his voice in my head saying, *When you are in trouble, communicate—clearly!*

So I called the military base again. And this time, I made sure they knew it was urgent. *Seymour Johnson, Cessna 68762 needs assistance.* Two seconds of silence and then a voice. *Cessna 68762, this is Seymour Johnson.* Finally, someone answered my call for help! I asked for a vector to the Johnson County airport (that's the nice way of saying I'm lost, please help), and the controller gave me the exact directions I needed. Along the way, he asked how I was doing and how much fuel I had. He apologized for not responding to my earlier calls for help. He told me they heard my earlier calls but didn't realize I was in trouble. He stayed on the radio with me for over thirty minutes, guiding me safely home. He saved my life that night, all because I remembered how to communicate the problem clearly.

You might be saying, *Well, Steve, I don't fly airplanes, so what's the point?* No matter what field you are in, you will crash as a leader if you don't communicate clearly. I thought I was reaching out for help the first two times I called Seymour Johnson over the radio, but since I didn't tell them what was actually going on, the military base ignored me. They didn't know I needed their help. Does that sound familiar? Miscommunication like this happens all the time in the workplace.

Communicating clearly to your employees means talking with them in terms they understand. If your employees are having difficulty understanding what you're trying to explain, it's time to change how you communicate. Listen to feedback from your employees (remember the chapter on listening? Quiet Now!). The questions they ask you can provide a useful starting point.

How you communicate something to your employees is just as important as what you say. In fact, the way you say something to anyone—whether your spouse, child, or friend—is just as important as what you're telling them. You can yell and condescend, or you can be calm and respectful; the choice is yours.

But if you want better results in your relationships, you better choose the latter over the former.

"You might be saying, Well, Steve, I don't fly airplanes, so what's the point? No matter what field you are in, you will crash as a leader if you don't communicate clearly."

Conversations with employees should always be helpful, clarifying, and encouraging. In all my years as a supervisor, I never once had to yell at an employee or hurt their pride. My goal has always been to lift them up and improve their performance. And it's worked. That's because employees respond positively when you treat them appropriately. Consider these two different ways of communicating with an employee about an assignment:

"I told you before how to prepare this letter. I can't believe you still don't get it! This is simple stuff. Are you sure you can handle this? Now look at my comments, fix it, and get this out today."

"The letter you prepared has some issues that need to be addressed. I made some edits to soften the wording since the topic involves a sensitive issue. We don't want to make negative judgments against the customer. Take a look at my comments and let me know what you come up with. Then re-prepare the letter for my signature. Thanks."

See the difference? The way you communicate has a big impact. In the first example, I'm just telling the employee they are inadequate. If I continue talking with them in this manner, I can expect little change and continued subpar performance. I'm not trying to help them or offer guidance on how they can improve. I'm just running them down. This approach creates a negative atmosphere and guarantees low performance from employees.

But in the second example, I focus on the issue at hand rather than the employee's ability. I provide feedback on their work without damaging their pride in the process. I communicate precisely what's wrong with the letter and provide feedback on the changes that need to be made. Ultimately, I want the employee to learn how to write the letter correctly, so I don't have to send it back to them with edits. To do that, I need to take the time to teach them how it needs to be done. So I provide comments and suggestions where changes need to be made and ask the employee to re-write those areas with my edits in mind. I don't want them just to do what I say; I want them to think about what they are doing and come up with ideas of their own, too. Communicating this way helps the employee learn and hopefully reduces the need for future edits. So not only does this approach fix the issue at hand, but it provides an opportunity for the employee to grow in their abilities. And as they improve their writing abilities, my job becomes easier.

Which method are you using when you communicate with employees? Are you focusing on their failure to do what you said, or are you building them up for success?

How you communicate matters and makes all the difference in your ability to lead effectively.

When I was in the Marine Corps, they taught us repeatedly that everyone is a leader. Even a private, the lowest rank in the military, is a leader. Even if you don't supervise anyone else in your position, you're still a leader. The Marines taught that you lead from wherever you are and teach others to do the same. History is full of privates taking leadership in battle and achieving victory. In my years with the government, I witnessed many non-supervisory employees step up and do outstanding things that yielded great results. When you give the employees you supervise feedback on how to be better and room to grow, you build leadership qualities in them. When you help your employees excel, you're helping yourself, too. And as your employees grow and lead in their responsibilities, your job becomes easier.

***

Communication is key to building your employees up to become leaders themselves. We've already discussed that how you communicate can either encourage your workers or tear them down. But the method you choose to communicate information to employees is just as important.

In today's workplace, supervisors can use email, text, phone calls or face-to-face meetings to communicate with their employees. Recently, during the COVID-19 pandemic we've also started to use more virtual meetings to communicate. They are similar to face-to-face, but not the same. I'll cover that later. You should know how to use each of these effectively in order to successfully lead your organization.

Let's start with the easiest: email. And I will include texting along with email since they are similar. Email can be your best friend or your worst enemy. It's great because you don't have to look the person you're communicating with in the eye. You don't have to hear them question you. You don't even have to know if they're available at the time. But there's one thing you must remember about emails. They never die. You can delete them, purge them, and take a hammer to the computer, yet copies of your emails will survive forever. When you send an email, it travels through several servers before reaching its destination. So despite your best efforts to delete them, copies of every email you send can be found and revived on each server the email has passed through. An email you sent ten years ago is still out there on a server somewhere, just waiting to be brought back to life. So be careful with the emails you send. Sooner or later, someone will try to revive an old email and allege that you did something wrong. If you follow my advice here, you will have nothing to worry about.

Some years ago, an employee in my office filed multiple Equal Employment Opportunity Commission (EEOC) complaints against me. I was making him do his job—and holding him accountable for results—and he didn't like it. So he tried to retrieve every single email I had ever sent him to prove what a horrible boss I was. Since emails never die, he was able to get all of them. And you know what those emails revealed? They were proof that I communicated professionally with him. In email after email, I offered him help and assistance to reach the standard of work I expected. And with a calm but stern tone, I confronted him on his numerous performance issues. Those emails were the best defense I could have possibly had. Not only did they exonerate me from the employee's allegations, but they convicted him of being in the wrong.

Emails are the best legal documentation you have as a supervisor. When I sent those emails all those years ago to this employee, I had no indication that I would someday be in court watching a judge read them. But I was so thankful in that moment that I adhered to professional standards in my emails, even though the employee emailing me didn't. In my case, the emails helped bring the truth to light, and it will for you, too.

So, be careful to use email wisely. Following these essential tips will help ensure that your emails will age gracefully.

First, don't send emails when you're mad. It's better to sleep on a situation if you're upset before hitting the send button. Remember, emails last forever. You don't want to send an angry email you'll quickly regret. Take some time away from the situation, and you will be surprised by how much the text and tone of your email will change. I've drafted emails in anger or frustration before, only to be shocked the following day at what I was going to send out! When you take time to calm down, you realize that you may have misread the intent of the person's email that made you angry in the first place. Or, you realize that what you were mad about isn't as bad as you initially thought. Clear your mind and your anger before sending out emails you'll regret later.

Second, don't capitalize words as if to "YELL" at your recipient. I see this sometimes in emails, and it isn't appropriate. Be polite and direct in your communication, but don't yell at the recipient.

Finally, respect your recipient's time by keeping emails short and sweet. Don't be that person who sends long-winded emails explaining something that could've been described in a few sentences. It wastes time, and that's everyone's most precious commodity. I make a point to re-read an email before I send it to catch errors and ensure my message isn't too long. If it is, I'll go back through it and take out what isn't needed.

Email is an excellent tool for communication, but only if you use it wisely. But, you'll often have to deal with situations that aren't best handled over email. When I want more of a personal conversation with an employee, I call them. A phone call is more personal than email, and most important, it's more private. I don't have to worry about my conversation being forwarded to others whom I don't want to be involved or worse. I can talk freely on the phone and feel somewhat more protected in my conversation.

Many sensitive discussions—personnel issues and ongoing litigation, for example—should be handled over the phone rather than through email. It's not that you need the privacy to talk trash about your workers or plot illegal activities. Phone calls are necessary for those times when you need privacy on a matter to openly discuss important information affecting your organization.

Of course, phone calls come in handy in lots of other ways, too. They're indispensable when email isn't working. It might sound ridiculous, but it happens more often than you think. I once spent hours going back and forth with an employee over email discussing a problem they were working on. I thought I was crystal clear in my emails about what she needed to do, but her responses left me dumbfounded. They made no sense. It was like I was writing to her in Chinese, and she was responding in German. I was becoming increasingly frustrated and was about to send her an angry reply when I came to my senses. I remembered a promise I made to myself long ago that I would not send emails in anger. And communicating over email in this situation wasn't working. So I finally did what I should have done hours earlier. I picked up the phone and called her. The issue was resolved in five minutes on the phone. And thankfully, she couldn't have been nicer about the whole situation.

Another time email failed me was when I had to ask my new boss, whom I had yet to meet, a question. I sent my email and a week went by with no response. So I sent a follow-up message. Still nothing. *Does he not like me?* I thought. *Am I annoying him?* Another week went by, and I still hadn't received a response from my boss. Now I was getting mad. I asked a colleague what the deal was with our new boss. "Oh, he doesn't like emails," my colleague told me. "Call him instead." So I picked up the phone and called my new boss. He acknowledged receiving my emails but stated he gets so many that he can't stay on top of them all. From then on, I avoided sending him emails and called him when I needed anything. When an email isn't working, a good old-fashioned phone call does the trick.

And when an issue is urgent, a phone call is by far the best way to communicate it. I know this seems obvious, but you'd be surprised. When there's an emergency, and people need to know information immediately, a phone call is the quickest way to report. A phone call conveys the urgency of a situation in a way that email can't. When an employee made threats against someone in my office, I got a phone call. When one of my employees was involved in a car crash, I got a call. When there was a significant crash in California featured on CNN, I got a phone call. When bad things happen, I want to know immediately. A phone call cuts through everything else going on and lets me know that an issue is too important to sit in my inbox.

I know younger generations prefer to use email for everything these days, but there will be times as a leader when picking up the phone and calling your employee, colleague, or boss is the wisest course of action. It's far more personal than email and allows you to convey emotions and protects privacy in a way that emails too often lack. And the best part? I guarantee that you can resolve misunderstandings more quickly over the phone than through email. So give it a try the next time a situation may be handled better over the phone.

Another method of communication is the good old-fashioned, face-to-face method. You need to look your employees in the eyes once in a while and talk to them in person. This allows you to get a better sense of the person you are dealing with. When you talk to someone face-to-face, you pick up on a wealth of nonverbal communication cues such as their demeanor, attitude, and sincerity.

When I was the division administrator in California, there were several branch offices in different parts of the state, hundreds of miles away from each other. Every six to eight weeks, I traveled to each office in person to visit the staff there. I sat down with the supervisors and other employees to chat about what was going on and how they were meeting their goals. These visits turned out to be one of the best things I did. No amount of emails or phone calls can take the place of in-person visits.

Now I know some of you might say that the use of virtual meetings via the Internet is just as good as in person. I disagree. They have their place as a communication tool. And I've used them quite a bit during the COVID-19 pandemic. But they are not as good as one-to-one, in-person meetings. They're not. I used them for well over a year and a half during the pandemic and held virtual meetings with employees and supervisors. These virtual methods are suitable, but not as good. You can rely on them for presentations, and short get-togethers, etc. But don't use them to substitute in-person meetings.

Let me give you one example. I have kids, I have a wife, and I love them. I miss them when I'm gone. It's good to see them virtually using my iPhone when I'm away on travel and they are thousands of miles away. Screen time with family though is never as good as seeing them in person. It's great when I can't be there, but it will never make a substitute for the real thing. The same applies at work. Don't be the virtual leader all the time. Show up in person; employees need to see their leader in person.

After the COVID-19 pandemic, I began meeting again with employees face-to-face instead of virtually—what a difference. Seeing people, conversing with them, laughing with them, is so much better than virtual. Sitting in my office and having a conversation with someone is just more valuable. There is a difference, and it's huge. As I was in my office recently, a new employee stopped by to talk, and we had a good conversation. I'm glad I was there to see him again and hear about how he's been since he returned from military duty. He was smiling and ready to get back to learning the job. This conversation would not have happened if I had relied solely on virtual meetings. This employee would not have spoken with me. I don't usually work with him on a daily basis. But because I was in the office, and so was he, he stopped in to talk. And what this demonstrated to me was that despite the pandemic, the time away, the difficulties, my folks were ready to go. He was motivated, talking up the job, and ready to get back to regular work. That impromptu conversation helped me see how well an employee was doing. He encouraged me that day in the office, and I hope I did the same for him.

Face-to-face, it can't be beat and it has the biggest impact with employees. Sending an email or making a phone call is easy, but in-person communication takes more commitment. And sometimes, it's the commitment that speaks volumes to the person you are trying to reach. Don't rely on virtual technology alone to keep you from the in-person, face-to-face leadership style. Doing so will limit your ability to lead and create good things in your workspace.

***

In-person communication has the power to change difficult situations. In 1942, U.S. Marines were fighting the Japanese on an island in the south Pacific called Guadalcanal. In October of 1942, Admiral William "Bull" Halsey had recently been placed in charge of the Guadalcanal Naval operations to replace another admiral who wasn't having much success. The Marines had been on the island for months fighting the best soldiers of Japan. Before Halsey's arrival, the U.S. Navy had lost a battle with the Japanese navy and fled for a few weeks to safety. The Marines were left to fight on with no air cover, little food, and dwindling ammunition. The Japanese, meanwhile, steadily resupplied the island with their best troops, determined to wipe out every last Marine on Guadalcanal.

Things weren't looking good for the Americans. The Marines were facing sleepless nights, constant enemy bombardment, and a shortage of supplies. When Admiral Halsey took charge of the Guadalcanal campaign, he immediately set out to re-supply the Marines with the materials they needed to fight. He met with the Marine commanders and listened to their concerns, assuring them of his support to win the battle. Guadalcanal was too important to lose, and only the Marines could win the battle for him. He needed to send a message and encourage the Marines to victory.

Imagine this for a moment. You've just been put in charge of overseeing a large, important project for your organization. But you've inherited a tough situation with the prior person in charge dismissed. As a result, the project is behind schedule and teetering on failure. Employee morale is suffering and if the project fails, it could wipe out your company. How do you inspire your employees to succeed? How do you turn the situation around? Send them a group text message? Hop on a video call? What would you do?

Admiral Halsey did something his predecessor did not do. He went in person to visit the Marines on Guadalcanal.[1] He traveled to Guadalcanal amid unrelenting combat and despite enemy snipers all around. He visited with the Marines on the front lines and witnessed the sites where fierce battles had recently raged. Everywhere he stopped, Marines and Army soldiers gathered around him and spoke to him one-on-one. They smiled and were encouraged by him. And Halsey could see for himself the tired, war-torn faces of the young men he was leading. The Marines responded to him because they felt he was one of them. The Marine commander on the island would later write, "On November 8, Admiral Halsey flew in like a wonderful breath of fresh air."

---

[1]   Wukovits, *Admiral "Bull" Halsey*, p. 105

Admiral Halsey did not have to visit Guadalcanal in person. He could have sent other officers to see the Marines. He could have just been satisfied with reading the daily activity briefings from the Marine officers on the island. But he did not. He wanted to show the young men fighting for their lives that he was with them. There was no better way to say this than to visit them in person, right where they were at.

There's no recording of a significant speech that Halsey made on Guadalcanal. Many Marines most likely were not able to leave their posts to meet him. But the message he sent couldn't have been more straightforward: I'm here with you, and we're going to win this battle together. As the Marines fought like hell against a determined enemy thousands of miles away from home, they didn't know if any of them would make it off the island alive. But they knew one thing: Admiral Halsey took the time to step off his comfy ship to be with them. He didn't need to say anything. His presence said it all. The Marines went on to win the battle of Guadalcanal, a huge victory for the United States in World War II.

Sometimes you need to make the sacrifice to show up in person like Admiral Halsey. Other times, you'll need to use all three of these communication methods we've covered. My daughter Kara was a Ph.D. student in charge of scheduling master's students to teach undergraduate course sections. All the master's students knew they had to commit to teaching these courses to receive their stipends from the university. Kara assigned the students to the classes they would teach via email. But there was one student who ignored her email. And despite several follow-ups, he never responded and confirmed he would teach. Worse, he didn't show up to teach his classes. Kara called me and asked for my advice. Have you tried calling him? I asked. She had, but he didn't answer his phone either. She called me again, stumped. When emails and phone calls don't work, what do you do?

I told Kara she needed to talk to this student in person. Even wait for him outside of one of his classes if necessary. And that's precisely what she did. She flagged him down as he was leaving a class one afternoon and asked to speak with him. Kara explained that she didn't want to turn him in to the university and threaten his stipend, but she wouldn't have any other choice if he continued to evade his responsibility. Show up and teach your class as you should, she told him. He acknowledged and said he would.

Kara didn't ask why the student didn't answer her many emails or phone calls. She didn't spend time hitting him over the head about it. She knew he received the emails and the calls and chose to ignore her. So she met him face-to-face and spoke to him as a leader. And you know what? That student never failed to show up to his teaching course again.

When it's obvious that other methods of communication aren't working, you need to talk to people face-to-face to get the job done. That's what a leader does. And when you focus on results rather than the person's shortcomings, you'll get the breakthrough you need. It can be nerve-wracking to confront people in person. Not everyone is a natural at this, but the good news is that it gets easier with practice. Commit yourself to use this powerful form of communication. You'll need it to be an effective, results-producing leader.

Becoming an effective communicator is essential to your success as a leader. While each communication method has its strengths and weaknesses, knowing which method to use in which circumstance and when to combine them will level up your communication skills. Most good leaders are excellent communicators, whether by email, phone, text, virtual, or in person. Practice using each form to its full advantage.

Chapter 17
Lessons in Communication
Key Takeaways and Applied Knowledge

Take it Further: Challenge yourself to implement one new idea from this chapter each week. Commit to broaden your use of each communication tool.

Chapter 18

A BETTER BANK ACCOUNT

Lessons in Employee Loyalty

Car problems are always frustrating, and a few years ago, I was having a miserable time trying to fix mine. I take pride in doing things myself, and over the years, I've learned how to perform a variety of minor car repairs. But on this particular day, I was trying to fix a big problem: replacing the engine mount on my SUV. It is just as tricky as it sounds and can be dangerous if it isn't done right. The engine must be raised and supported while the mount that holds it in place is switched out for a new one. And things were not going my way. I spent the whole day trying to get the old engine mount off! By late afternoon, with no progress made, I was mad, frustrated, and exhausted. I was sitting on my garage floor in complete defeat when suddenly, someone walked in unannounced.

This person better not try to sell me something, I thought. Instead, I heard a friendly, "Hi neighbor!" It was my neighbor from across the street whom I hadn't met yet. "I've seen you working on your car all day and wondered if you might need some help." Boy did I. I readily accepted, and before I knew it, my neighbor looked at my engine mount and advised me what I needed to do to get it off. A few hours later, I was able to get the old mount off and replace it with a new one. Not only did my neighbor help me fix my car that day, but he also helped me recover my pride. And that started a friendship between us that continues to this day.

When was the last time you helped one of your employees with a personal matter? Maybe they need to adjust their hours for childcare or take some time off for a family matter. Perhaps they want to leave a little early one day to see their son play baseball.

Whatever it might be, helping your workers out when they need it is crucial to building employee loyalty. When you show your employees you care about them as a person and not just as a worker, you cultivate a healthy environment where employees are appreciative and content at work. And when your employees feel valued, they will be loyal to you. They will be there for you when you need them. They may even show up on a day off just because they want to help.

When I worked for the government, overtime pay was not permitted. Most of the time, the agency had no money for it, so we avoided it as much as possible. But sometimes, I needed people to work on weekends to investigate a crash. Sometimes I needed them to work late and finish up assignments or be in the office when they weren't required to be there. And each time I needed employees to work overtime for no pay, they did it out of loyalty to me. You see, you often get back what you give to others.

When my neighbor helped me with my car repair, he actually helped himself. The goodwill he showed to me that day came back to him too, but not because it was owed to him.

You see, goodwill is not about tracking what someone owes you or what you owe them for the nice thing they did for you. It's about how you view that person and your willingness to go the extra mile for them. I'll go the extra mile to help my neighbor with projects he's working on at his house not because I owe it to him but because I appreciate how he helped me in my time of need.

The friendship I have with my neighbor is a perfect example of what author Stephen Covey identifies as an emotional bank account. In his book, *The 7 Habits of Highly Effective People*, Mr. Covey explains that this bank account represents the amount of trust that's been built up in a relationship, whether between friends, spouses, or coworkers.[1] When the trust is high, one can call upon it in times of need. When the bank account is low or overdrawn, everything becomes more difficult. Tensions in the relationship or friendship increase, and every word can become a minefield. According to Mr. Covey, small discourtesies, little unkindnesses, and minor forms of disrespect can all cause large withdrawals from your account. But on the other hand, seeking to understand someone,

---

1   Stephen R. Covey, *The 7 Habits of Highly Effective People*, 1989, p. 188

attending to the little things, and keeping commitments can make major deposits into this account.

Mr. Covey could not have been more correct. Even the smallest of discourtesies can significantly damage a relationship. To this day, I still remember the time when a supervisor I looked up to disrespected me. We were both at a large regional meeting, and this supervisor was leading a group discussion. The supervisor knew me, but he hadn't even acknowledged my presence in the group. Here was his chance to make things right, I thought, as he came to each table to pass along some meeting work-sheets. Instead, he looked right at me, did not say a word, handed me the sheets, and moved on. I was offended. I always acknowledged my colleagues when I saw them at meetings like this. How much effort does it take to say "Hi"? Since he could not even take the time to do that, I never trusted him again. His bank account was overdrawn with me forever. I know this sounds petty, but it is the little things that often make or break relationships.

Whether we signed up for one or not, we all have this bank account. Each time you do something nice for your employees, like buying lunch for the office, bringing in do-nuts on a Friday, or saying a friendly hello every morning, you deposit into that emotional bank account. Every time you show kindness or keep a commitment, you make a deposit into this bank account. The gesture doesn't have to be elaborate or expensive. In fact, most have little to no cost at all. It could be as simple as letting everybody go home early the day before a holiday. What matters here is that you show goodwill toward those you supervise.

You must do things that continually make positive deposits into this emotional bank account because the account will naturally get drawn down, and you don't want it to go to zero or worse, a negative balance. Have you ever seen a marriage that's run out of goodwill? Spouses start doing the bare minimum for each other. They become so comfortable in the routine that they take each other for granted. They stop investing in their emotional bank accounts. Trust levels deteriorate, and little things blow up into big things when that happens. Arguments occur over the most minor issues and the marital foundation begins to crumble. And when the storm comes, the relationship ultimately falls apart. The bank account is overdrawn; it's empty. There is nothing left to give on either side. Each side stopped adding to the bank account somewhere along the way. The results are terrible, yet are sadly predictable.

The same thing can happen with supervisors and employees. I've seen supervisors removed from their positions because their working relationships with employees became so toxic. Over the years, these supervisors continued to demand more and more of their employees without ever showing their appreciation. And guess what? The emotional bank account quickly went bankrupt. Not surprisingly, the employees became bitter. They were no longer willing to go the extra mile. So when these offices faced challenges, there were no employees who were willing to go above and beyond to help the supervisors. The employees hated their boss for refusing to show appreciation for their work, and the boss hated the employees. After numerous employee complaints, upper management stepped in and removed the supervisors from their positions.

If you always ask, ask, ask and demand, demand, demand from your employees without ever showing your appreciation for them, you will create an atmosphere of bitterness that will make life miserable for everyone. People won't stick around long working for a boss who doesn't appreciate their worth. When this happens employees have one of two options: they can flee, or they can take their boss down. If you are bankrupt with goodwill towards your employees, you'll soon find yourself with no team around you at all. Everyone will have left for better jobs, or if not, you may find yourself out of one.

You will face plenty of difficult times on the job as a leader, and having a dedicated team around you to support you and carry out your vision is essential to successfully navigating these challenges. Making this small investment will help you attract good people who are willing to go above and beyond to help you when you need it. And trust me, you absolutely will.

The famous UCLA basketball coach John Wooden, who won a record ten NCAA titles, said, "Little things make big things happen." One of the little things he taught his players was how to tie their shoes properly. It sounds like a small thing, but it's obviously important so his players don't trip on their shoelaces all over the court. But also a good-fitting shoe, tied properly, helps prevent blisters that could keep one from playing. And the team can't be the best unless everyone plays.

The same thing is true in any workplace. It's the little things you do for your employees that make big things happen. These don't have to be grandiose or expensive, but they need to come from the heart. I encourage time off during the holidays, and I cover the tough days like Christmas Eve and New Year's Eve so they can enjoy time with their family. These aren't big or expensive things for me to do. Some of these actions are really easy. But each one makes a crucial deposit into that emotional bank account.

When employees feel valued, they are willing to go above and beyond to help you when needed. I've never had trouble getting folks to work overtime or on weekends. Since our agency couldn't demand overtime work, my employees could've told me no—and there would have been nothing I could do about it. Thankfully, it never got to that point because someone was always willing to step up and help me out. Showing your employees how much you appreciate their work may seem like a small thing at the moment, but it will prove to be a worthwhile investment for you.

"When employees feel valued, they are willing to go above and beyond to help you when needed."

Now let me show you one of the easiest, simplest ways to make deposits into this emotional bank account. I've given you some examples already, but this one has a no-excuse clause. That means there is no excuse on your part if you don't use this. It does not have a financial cost. It does not negatively affect the job in any way. This does not cost you anything to use. But it will pay you big dividends. If you are not doing this, you are letting thousands of goodwill bank account dollars go to waste. Are you ready for it?—then say "thank you." Say "thank you." Say "thank you" when your employee does a good job. Say "thank you" when your employee makes a customer happy. Say "thank you" when your employee goes the extra mile on a project that makes you look really good. Say "thank you" when your employee worked through a difficult day and did a great job. Say "thank you" when your employee covers the office on a holiday.

Do you get the point? Saying "thank you" is the best, easiest, no-cost way to deposit into the goodwill account. In fact, I find ways to say "thank you" to my employees as much as possible. They don't have to do something outstanding; many times, it's the little things they do. Remember, little things make big things happen. I tell them "thank you" in person for doing a good job. I put "thank you" in my emails. And my "thank you" tells them I appreciate and acknowledge their good work. Many problems could be solved with employee/supervisor relationships if someone would just say "thank you." And if you look close enough, there is always something to be thankful for with your employees.

As I wrote this chapter, it reminded me of the supervisors I had during my government career. I had a good working relationship with most, and I was always willing to do more for them. They said "thank you" when I did a good job. Some would buy a round of drinks when we were out on travel. Others would bring in treats when we were having a meeting. They made deposits to that emotional bank account. And I was loyal to them because they made me feel appreciated. It was not big things; it was the little things they did to say "thank you" to me that counted the most.

People don't want to work for a boss who takes their work for granted. They want to be in an environment where their supervisor shows them that their work is valued and appreciated. When you take time to do the little things for your employees, you cultivate a healthy work environment where people will actually want to go above and beyond.

By doing this, you'll keep employee complaints to a minimum, and you will create goodwill with them. I've had very few complaints from employees over the years, and I attribute this to the goodwill investments I made. Now, showing your employees goodwill is not a guarantee that you will never have problems. But when you do, facing them with a bank account that is full versus empty is a much better position to be in.

I covered other things that make big deposits into this emotional bank account in earlier chapters of this book. I covered being honest with those you supervise, listening to employees and being patient with them. I covered treating your employees with respect and dignity, even when they are clearly wrong. Each time you do one of these items you are making a deposit into your bank account. And it's something you should be doing every day. These things don't cost you much, but they will cost you dearly if you fail to do them.

Investing in an emotional bank account is crucial if you want to attract and retain high-performing, motivated employees to work for your organization. Take the time to show your workers you appreciate them and everything they do to further your team's mission. As the famous saying goes, people may forget what you said and what you did, but they will never forget how you made them feel. Employees will remember the times your actions made them feel valued and appreciated. And when you need their help, they will be willing to go the extra mile to help you out.

The little things you do to show employees your gratitude will help you achieve better results. So go ahead and bring in donuts this week. Let everyone go home early before the next holiday. Show appreciation to your employees for the hard work they do for you. By helping your employees, you're helping yourself.

Chapter 18
Lessons in Employee Loyalty
Key Takeaways and Applied Knowledge

Take it Further: Identify one small actionable step you can take immediately after reading this chapter to show appreciation to your employees.

Chapter 19

HARDTACK PLEASE

Lessons in Employee Satisfaction

'm not talking about tact, that sensitivity you need when telling someone bad news. No, this chapter is about *hardtack* or tack, defined as

> *"A simple type of biscuit or cracker made from flour, water, and sometimes salt. Hardtack is inexpensive and long-lasting. It is used for sustenance in the absence of perishable foods, commonly during long sea voyages, land migrations, and military campaigns."*

Before you think I've lost my cracker talking about tack, stick with me here, okay? There's an important leadership message for you and me in the simple food called tack.

Tack was widely used as food for union and confederate soldiers in the Civil War. Since bread is easily perishable, armies were unable to use it to feed their men. Tack made a decent replacement, and it was the closest thing the soldiers had to real bread.

During the Civil War, General Grant was known to ride on horseback for hours to check in on his army, reconnoiter enemy lines, and visit his fellow generals in the area. On one of his rides, during the battle of Vicksburg, General Grant encountered a group of his own Union soldiers, who started shouting at him. "Hardtack, hardtack, hardtack!" they yelled at him.[1]

Imagine you are General Grant for a moment. You're in front of a group of soldiers who are demanding more tack. You're in the middle of the Civil War with the fate of the country hanging in the balance. You are most likely exhausted, working all day and strategizing army movements well into the night. General Grant is responsible for thousands of soldiers, not to mention the outcome of the war that hangs over his head. He's pushed to the limit. What would your response be to the soldiers' demands for more tack?

There are many ways General Grant could have answered these soldiers. "You're eating meat and poultry," he could have told them, "You aren't starving." Or, "The war is in the balance and the country will fall if we lose. You're worried about tack right now?" He could have blown up in their faces. "How dare you question me on such a silly request in the middle of war!! I should have you all court-martialed!!!" He could have said any number of things. The soldiers' request was a small one when many other concerns took precedence. General Grant could have ignored it and carried on with his ride. But he didn't.

---

1   Konecky & Konecky, *The Personal Memoirs of Ulysses S. Grant*, p. 310

He replied to the soldiers saying he would get them more hardtack.

These soldiers were winning battles for General Grant. They were the heart and soul of his army. They suffered and died each day. They were taking the brunt of an awful war, and kept at it day after day. In the big picture, asking for more tack was low on the priority scale. But General Grant got it for them.

What does this have to do with leadership? Sometimes your frontline workers will ask you for something that seems like a big deal to grant. As the leader, you could say there are many other priorities that require your attention. You could remind them of all of the other things you give them. Or you could get mad at them and lose your temper. You could ... but you should think about it.

The Union soldiers didn't *need* tack to survive. It was more of a luxury than a requirement. But General Grant had a heart for his men and didn't take offense at their request. How do you think those soldiers felt about him after they got what they asked for? How do you think they fought for him? The general spent very little money and effort getting these men their tack, but got a big return for his money in the form of dedication and respect.

Just like General Grant, have some tack when dealing with your employees. Don't take offense when they ask for things that aren't absolutely necessary, but show them some empathy. I remember a staff conference years ago where a few trucking investigators—who spent most days driving around visiting trucking companies—asked management for cars with cruise control. You see, back then, most cars didn't have it (shocking, I know). The investigators weren't rude or condescending with their request. They simply asked for something that would help make their job easier. Yet the response they received from management was, "You already have cruise control, it's called your foot. Use it." That was like an iron fist in the face to these investigators. Such a heartless response makes employees feel that they aren't worth much to the organization, and creates resentment in the ranks.

"Don't take offense when they ask for things that aren't absolutely necessary, but show them some empathy."

Some supervisors view employee requests as inherently negative. They take offense at employees for insinuating their leadership is lacking and bristle at claims they aren't providing their employees what they need. This is the wrong way to look at requests from your workers. While requests certainly can be negative and critical of the leadership, that doesn't mean each and every one is. Many times employees are simply asking for something that they truly need in the workplace. You may need to say no sometimes, and that's okay. But do it in a professional manner that doesn't denigrate the employee for the asking. And think of the cost-benefit ratio when deciding whether to spend a little to gain a lot in return.

An office manager whom I supervised was unwilling to purchase flashlights as her employees requested. Why? She reasoned that flashlights weren't absolutely necessary for employees to do their jobs. So the employees came to me to ask why they couldn't get the flashlights they needed to conduct truck inspections. While most inspections were done during the day in good lighting conditions, there were exceptions, and a flashlight could assist with the task. Flashlights are not expensive, and the employees could have purchased their own. But it was job-related, and it seemed like such a small request. I did not think the employees were trying to take advantage of the agency or my office. So I acted.

I spoke with their supervisor and advised her that requests within reason and with minimal costs, like flashlights, should be approved. I wanted my employees to feel that they are important and that their requests, no matter how small, are heard. And if that means buying each of them flashlights, then so be it. She agreed and purchased the flashlights. It was a small thing, sort of like General Grant getting some crackers for his soldiers. But it had a big impact. The next time I saw those employees they thanked me for the new equipment. I could hardly believe they were so excited to get a small flashlight, but they were. That light reminded them that their leadership was willing to listen to their concerns and cared about them. Those employees turned out to be loyal and productive for my agency. I'm sure it was not all attributable to the flashlights we bought them. But it sure did not hurt.

Throughout my career I always tried to get tack for my employees when they asked. I've been asked to purchase paper calendars, flashlights, items for the cars, better laptop bags, phones, MIFI devices, and the list goes on and on. None of these requests were absolutely necessary. I knew that even though such requests seemed small to me, it meant something to them. And when I could provide a little more support to them, for little cost, I did it. General Grant did not get his soldiers tack because they needed it. He did it, like I did, because it was an investment in his soldiers. An investment initially costs you money since you have to spend something to make them. But they pay off in the long run, usually many times over. The key is knowing when to make low-cost investments that will pay back big dividends, and when to avoid spending money on foolish requests. It's a balance you must weigh with each request.

I've been on the other side asking for tack and it hurt when small requests were denied. One such item my peers and I had an issue with was our iPhones. We were issued iPhones for our jobs, which required us to constantly check them even when off-duty and on weekends. I understood

I had an important position and it came with the job. I accepted that fact. I understood that I had to check for important emails constantly each day. But in order for me to check my email I had to type in a twelve-digit password each time. That's right, a twelve-digit password that contained at least one uppercase letter, one lowercase letter, a special character and one number. And oh, by the way, this had to get changed every sixty to ninety days. This was crazy considering that the iPhones were equipped with touch ID. But our agency refused to allow use of the touch ID feature.

You can imagine how painful it was to constantly check email with a twelve-digit password every day. The agency was repeatedly asked why we could not use the touch ID to make our lives easier. On one such call, a person from our IT department stated the reason why touch ID was not allowed. He stated that our fingerprints could potentially be lifted off a glass at a restaurant and then copied and used to open our iPhones. It was a security thing. Our small cracker request ran head-on into Internet security. And we would lose that fight every time. This basically communicated to me that our IT department did not care. It was easier for them to say no. They did not realize how important it was to me and others who had to open that phone many times each day.

This is a good example of how to look at tack requests. We were asking for these crackers so we could do our jobs better. We were asking for tack to check our email more frequently and easily. It was not absolutely necessary since we had been putting in that twelve-digit passcode for some time. But it sure would help morale and result in more emails being checked. Listen when your employees ask for crackers, especially when it will help them do their jobs better. I get it, our IT department did not want to take the time to evaluate the use of touch ID. It would cost them something and they could be blamed if a security incident occurred. But you have to have balance, and you have to consider your employees. Eventually, the iPhone policy was changed to the relief of myself and many others.

Employees work hard for you. Show them some tack by evaluating requests with their needs in mind. Evaluate the pros and cons of each request and the impact it will likely have on employee satisfaction. You don't have to approve every request, but make sure your employees know they are valued and their needs are taken seriously. Employees remember the little things you do for them, like buying flashlights or allowing them to use touch ID on their iPhones. I still am thankful for that unknown person who allowed me to open my iPhone with touch ID. So when you get the chance to do so, show them some tack.

Chapter 19
Lessons in Employee Satisfaction
Key Takeaways and Applied Knowledge

Take it Further: Identify one actionable step you can take after reading this chapter. Do your employees have the tools they need to be their best? Are there some employee requests that you may want to reconsider after reading this chapter?

Chapter 20

STUDY TIME

Lessons in Job Knowledge

When I was in my twenties, I decided to learn how to fly. Ever since I was a kid, I dreamed of piloting an airplane someday, flying high above the clouds and seeing the world far below. I remember how in awe I was at the jet airplanes I would see when my family took me to the airport to pick up friends or relatives who would come to visit. I would watch the big jets take off and land, and I was so enamored with flight. I knew I had to be a pilot someday, even if it was not going to be flying a jet.

The first plane I trained in was a single-engine Cessna 152. It's about the smallest plane one can fly, with only two seats and a small cargo area in the back. I quickly realized one thing as I began taking flying lessons—I better know my stuff. And knowing everything about the plane I was flying was essential. So I purchased an operator's manual for the aircraft I would be piloting. I studied every inch of that manual from start to finish. I read everything I would need to know about successfully flying the plane. I learned how to check the oil and identify the operating controls in the cockpit. I learned about the aircraft's stall speeds, fuel capacities, weight and balance, takeoff and landing speeds, and much more. Knowing such details was crucial to flying the plane accurately—and safely.

When flying an airplane, there is no substitute for knowing it inside and out. It took me months to make my way through Cessna's manual. But it was time well spent. The knowledge I gained from hours of careful study gave me the confidence to fly that plane and react well in emergency situations. Later on, I flew different aircraft and had to repeat the same careful study again and again for each aircraft. What I learned about one plane was not automatically transferable to the other. This left me at square one for each new aircraft I was eager to fly. The same is true for your profession.

Simply put, you have to know what you're doing to lead others successfully. The employees you supervise will rely on your knowledge to help them do their job better. For many years of my career with the federal government, I led employees who interpreted and enforced federal safety regulations. There was a seemingly endless amount of rules and myriad interpretations of those regulations. My employees had to know them, and so did I. I made it my goal to study and understand the regulations better than my employees. When they had questions, I could answer them. When they needed guidance, I was able to provide it. When they needed to discuss technical matters, I could participate. And when they ran into difficult circumstances, I was able to help. To lead my employees in these matters meant I had to know about their work. Without that knowledge, I would have been lost—and so would they.

*"Simply put, you have to know what
you're doing to lead others successfully."*

I always enjoy it when my employees view me as someone who can help them as they tackle projects and tasks. I enjoy talking about their work and discussing technical questions with them. I enjoy sharing information and watching them learn. The best part is that I get to know more about their work in the process. These conversations wouldn't be possible if I were clueless about their jobs and responsibilities. Having a strong knowledge base of my employees' job responsibilities enabled constructive communication with them. It revealed to me areas where more training might be necessary or where policies needed to improve. I wouldn't try to fly a plane without reading its flight manual. And I wouldn't try to lead others without knowing as many of the aspects of their job as I should.

Cultivating this leadership knowledge takes time and discipline. The larger and more complex the work, the more challenging it becomes. You need to know enough about the work employees perform to interact with them and provide leadership. Reading up on topics and issues they deal with and spending time sharing your insights with them is key to effective leadership.

When I became the division administrator in California, I began supervising individuals who worked at the southern border crossing with Mexico. I had never supervised such employees before. And although some of their work was familiar to me, many other aspects of it were not. I wasn't familiar with how they interacted with the Customs and Border Protection agents at the ports. I didn't know how they selected vehicles for inspection or how they operated with the California Highway Patrol. And I knew nothing about how they worked with the Mexican trucking industry to communicate agency regulations and policies. I just did not have much experience with work at the southern border.

Yet, despite this lack of knowledge and experience, I found myself responsible for leading these employees. I felt out of place, and I worried I was in over my head. You may find yourself in a similar position supervising a group of employees whose work you don't fully understand. While it can feel scary and overwhelming, the good news is that a lack of knowledge is something you can overcome. There is a way forward in these situations: learning.

I knew I needed to learn more about my employees' work, but I had a lot of other duties that consumed my time. I was responsible for employees who conducted investigations of trucking companies. I was leading subordinate supervisors and managers in various program and personnel matters. I had to manage relationships with state officials and was ultimately responsible for millions of federal grant dollars provided to the state of California. I was also the final approving official on federal civil-enforcement actions that assessed penalties against companies for violating federal safety laws. Needless to say, there were a lot of moving parts inherent in my position demanding my attention.

Despite the challenges, I committed to learning more about the operations at the southern border. I traveled to our offices on the border as often as I could and spent time interacting with the employees and managers. I would pepper them with questions about their work and daily tasks. I wanted to educate myself about their jobs and responsibilities and how I could best lead them. And it worked. I used the knowledge I gained during these visits to successfully lead the program to even better results.

Even though I had little knowledge of southern border operations when I started my California job, my commitment to learning more about it enabled me to gain substantial knowledge quickly. And as I spent time speaking with and learning more about my employees and their responsibilities, I gained the confidence to lead them effectively. Knowledge is power. When you have it, you will feel confident to lead. But it isn't always handed to you on a silver platter. You have to commit to the learning process and make the time in your schedule to accomplish it.

***

There are a few types of knowledge needed in supervision. First, you need technical knowledge of the direct job you supervise. The ability to converse with and assist those who report to you is essential to effective leadership. And as a leader, there will be a lot you need to know. Throughout my government career, I had to answer regulatory questions. This required technical knowledge of the federal safety and hazardous material regulations. My agency initially provided me training in these areas but it was not sufficient. The regulations change, new rules are added, some are removed and new interpretations are routinely issued. In addition to the regulations, the agency policies and procedures were just as important, as they spelled out how the agency would enforce and penalize violations of its regulations. I had to discipline myself to read and stay current on this ever-changing landscape of rules.

Regardless of how high I advanced in my organization, I always maintained my proficiency in regulatory knowledge. I needed this technical knowledge to lead those below me and answer questions from those we regulated. That knowledge gave me an edge and it helped me to succeed. Such knowledge took me years to cultivate and required time and energy to keep current. It will for you too. But technical knowledge isn't something you magically wake up with one day. It takes time and commitment to learning the ins and outs of your chosen field and position. And you need that knowledge to lead effectively.

You don't have to work in a regulatory setting for this to be important to your success. I have a cousin who owns a shoe business and sells quality products to his customers. He's a good businessman who's done well over many years. What impresses me the most about him is his knowledge of his craft. He knows everything one can know about his line of work. I would listen as he spoke with customers and explained to them about their shoes. He described the characteristics of the soles and the shoe materials and how that would affect their walk. He could answer questions about why a shoe was hurting someone's feet or how it was causing them to trip. By asking a customer a few questions, he knew what would be a good comfortable shoe for them. And throughout his career, he's continued to take training and acquire new skills in his business such as becoming a certified orthotic shoemaker. He knows his stuff and provides his customers with the information they will not get elsewhere.

You also need what I call general knowledge. As I supervised more employees, it became clear to me that I couldn't be an expert in every area. For example, my office had a hazardous materials specialist, Don, who was second to none. He knew more about that particular topic than anyone else in the private sector or federal government. Don taught industry classes on hazardous materials and cargo tank compliance and had deep technical knowledge of those complex and lengthy regulations. He was the best, and as the leader, I was happy to let him be the expert in this area. There was no way I could ever surpass Don's knowledge of hazardous materials.

Even though I couldn't be the technical expert on hazardous materials, I could still effectively lead Don in his duties. All that was required of me was to have basic knowledge and understanding of his job. I made an effort to learn as much as I could from him when we talked. At times I would pull my regulations book out and follow along as he explained why he was citing a particular regulation against a company. I asked Don lots of questions to further my understanding and also to ensure he was solid in his reasoning. Most importantly, I listened to him. I took the time to talk with him when he was in the office. These actions helped me gain general knowledge about his area of expertise that enabled me to supervise him properly. And it worked well. When Don retired, he told me he appreciated the way in which I had led him.

You can do the same. You don't have to shy away from leading others because you don't share their level of expertise. It might feel overwhelming at first, but start taking those steps to develop a better understanding of what your employees do and how they do it. Take the time to talk with them and learn about their job and day-to-day responsibilities. And don't be afraid to ask them questions. This will help you gain more general knowledge and help you lead your employees to bigger and better outcomes.

The final type of knowledge I believe you need to supervise others effectively is business knowledge. You need to know the current trends in your line of work and stay up to date on the latest developments affecting it. Leaders in the technology industry spend hours analyzing the latest news in their field. As an avid fan, I find it fascinating to read weekly blogs and news stories detailing the new technology products coming to market. Leaders in the military study the latest weapon technology and read up on tactics being used by other countries. Leaders in healthcare study new ways of delivering the latest medical advances in treating illnesses.

Acquiring business knowledge isn't just for leaders of large corporations. I've known leaders of small companies that study trends in their industry to stay competitive. It revolves around knowledge of what your company is doing and what others in your field are doing as well. It's about understanding where things are today and where they may be headed tomorrow. In my later years with the government, I read articles and studies about new safety technologies that have tremendous potential to improve safety for commercial trucks and buses. I became convinced it was the future in my field of safety enforcement. At every opportunity, I preached the message that technology would be the giant safety leap forward for the agency. I still believe that, and I hope to live to see that happen.

"Acquiring business knowledge isn't just for leaders of large corporations. I've known leaders of small companies that study trends in their industry to stay competitive."

How do you get this business knowledge I'm talking about? It's simple—read. Throughout my career, I have always made time to read. It enabled me to become the leader I am today. Educate yourself as much as you can whether through work manuals, organization policies, industry publications, or news articles. Stay current on changes in your field and keep a reliable reference system to find relevant information. Scheduling time to discover new information is essential. Without it, it's too easy to get caught up in the seemingly endless list of tasks demanding your attention. I scheduled a few hours every Friday to scan new data that came in during the week. It kept me updated on every policy change and interpretation, allowing me to become well-versed in new regulations before they were implemented. And when I ran out of new reading material, I reviewed materials I needed to sharpen up on.

It's essential to be prepared for your responsibilities as a leader. There's no excuse for being lost. Job knowledge—technical, general, and business—plays a big part in your success as a leader. It'll give you the confidence to lead your employees and help you understand their work. Take the time to cultivate your job knowledge. Schedule time to talk with your employees and learn more about their work. Prioritize reading and stay up to date on the latest developments in your field so you will be well-prepared to lead. This requires an investment of your most precious resource—time. Remember, as discussed in chapter 1 (Santa Claus is What?), there are no free lunches. To gain leadership skills you must invest the time and energy it takes to develop them. Trust me, it's an investment that will pay you back a hundredfold.

Knowledge and information are your friends as a leader. Assess where you need more technical, general, or business knowledge in your current job. Then make a plan on what you need to do to get it. It's never too late to start learning more about the business you work in each day. Where are your knowledge gaps? What disciplines can you implement to make the time commitment necessary to study and learn? Leaders know their stuff, they must to be successful. The information is out there, waiting for you to grab it. Go get it. That's what leaders do.

Chapter 20
Lessons in Job Knowledge
Key Takeaways and Applied Knowledge

Take it Further: Set a specific knowledge goal inspired by the chapter for your career and outline a plan to achieve it.

Chapter 21

HOLD YOUR FIRE

Lessons in Self-Control

There's an old proverb that says it's easier to take control of a city than it is one's tongue. The words you say can heal or destroy. They can project calm or panic. They can cool down a situation or set the house on fire. And as a leader, the words you choose can lead to a harassment charge, an Equal Employment Opportunity Commission (EEOC) court hearing, or the possible loss of your job. Your tongue can get you in a lot of trouble. Such a powerful tool must be controlled and used wisely.

Nothing will test your ability to control your tongue more than being a supervisor. All it takes is one word—seriously, just one word—for a complaint to be filed on you and send you packing. I've seen many competent supervisors make the bad mistake of failing to control their words carefully and it sank their careers.

"Controlling your tongue and speaking wisely isn't something that comes naturally to us. It requires practice, discipline, and most of all, patience."

Being angry can create a dangerous situation by allowing an uncontrolled tongue to cause a lot of damage. Anger charges the tongue and gets it ready to fire off hurtful words and allegations against others. It aims its venom at the target of your ire and unloads with verbal insults, harsh sarcasm, and pain. And once the tongue has unleashed its fury, there's no taking it back. We've all had our moments like this. In your personal life, this can destroy relationships. In your professional life, it can ruin your career. While friends and family may forgive you, the workplace often won't.

As I write this chapter, a U.S. naval commander was removed from his post commanding an aircraft carrier because he sent an unclassified letter to top Navy leadership pleading for help with an outbreak of COVID-19 on his ship. The Navy, incensed with the commander's poor lack of judgment in sending an unclassified letter to top officials, fired the guy. The acting secretary of the Navy was then sent to speak to the ship's crew who suddenly found themselves without a leader. Instead of reassuring them and rallying support, he disparaged their departing leader by saying he was "too naive or too stupid to command a ship." And guess what? A few days later, the acting secretary was asked to resign for his comments.[1]

1   "Acting Navy secretary says ousted captain leaked concerns to media, or was 'too naive or too stupid to command a ship,'" Washington Post, April 6, 2020.

"Navy upholds firing of carrier captain who warned of coronavirus," Politico, June 19, 2020.

"Modly Resigns As Acting Navy Chief After Firing Warship Skipper And

Controlling your anger is easier said than done. I've become angry at employees in my office for something they did or didn't do, and it's tempting to have them report to you and unleash your anger on them. However tempting it might be, this is never the wise solution. Learning how to control your anger and frustration in a professional setting takes time. I get as mad as the best of them, but my employees rarely know it. That's because over the course of my career I've learned how to control my anger by measuring my words carefully. I think before I speak so I can craft the message I want to convey minus the harmful daggers that wound others. I've worked hard to ensure that I'm not transferring my anger to my tongue to verbally beat up someone I'm unhappy with. It's about training the tongue to work for you and not against you.

Some leaders try to justify their outbursts by saying they can't control their anger. Others say the circumstance demanded such a reaction. But none of these excuses are true. You are either in control of your tongue or your tongue is in control of you. And as the leader, you set the tone and example for those you lead. You are expected to succeed in this mission of controlling your words and emotions even when others have lost control of theirs. There is no "I can't do this" or "I shouldn't have done that" or "Oh, I didn't mean what I said." Those excuses are for people who don't lead. They try to excuse or justify their

---

Calling Him Stupid," NPR, April 7, 2020.

inability to control themselves as a way to deflect blame for not being more careful and in control of their words. If you do this as a leader, you will not be one for long.

> *"Controlling your anger is easier said than done. I've become angry at employees in my office for something they did or didn't do, and it's tempting to have them report to you and unleash your anger on them."*

One of the most important instructions I give my subordinates is to discuss things with me first before elevating it to the next level of leadership. If I feel the need to raise an issue with top leadership, then I will be the one to do so. Not only does this practice give my team a chance to solve our own problems first before taking them to someone else to solve, but it also prevents my bosses from dealing with unnecessary issues. They've got enough work as it is. I'm not going to bother them with questions and problems that I can solve.

I was out of the office on a trip when one of my employees, acting as a supervisor on my behalf, sent a routine question to my boss without so much as a heads-up to me. When I read the email that was sent, I exploded in frustration. The last thing my boss needed was to deal with a question from my team that I could've quickly answered.

So how did I respond to that supervisor? Chewed him out, screaming and yelling about how many times I've told him not to do that? How he's been here long enough and should know better? How I can't understand how he doesn't know this by now? I said all of these things in my mind, but none of them made it to my tongue. When I'm angry, my tongue stays disengaged until I'm ready to give it orders. And by the time I discussed the issue with the employee, I was calm. I had taken the time to settle down and express myself without getting mad. In fact, I was able to look at the situation with a little more empathy. This employee was a hard worker and a great guy. I knew he didn't intend to make me upset. When we spoke, I gave him a pointed reminder why all such questions were to go through me first. That's it. No yelling or screaming was involved.

Simply taking time to calm down when you're angry works wonders. In his book Thinking Fast and Slow, author Daniel Kahneman describes how your mind works fast and it works slow. He terms these two systems working in the human mind as System 1 and System 2. System 1 is fast, intuitive and emotional, with little or no effort and no sense of voluntary control. An example would be seeing a black bear in the woods or orienting one to the source of a sudden sound. System 1 would make a quick analysis and decision on what to do. System 1 is absolutely need-ed, it's innate and helps us perceive the world around us. System 2 on the other hand, is slower, more deliberative, and more logical. It involves more mental activity, such as solving a math problem. It is associated with agency, choice and concentration. System 2 monitors System 1 and for example, would keep one polite when they are angry. To tap into the benefits of System 2 one needs to slow things down so more deliberate, thoughtful actions can take place when warranted.

Quickly responding to a situation when you're upset short-circuits your brain into fight mode and lets your emotions get the best of you. The anger takes over and wants to use the pain and frustration you feel to lash out at others. For example, if someone throws you under the bus during a meeting at work, it's natural to want to immediately confront them. When you see them in the hallway ten minutes later, you really want to give them a piece of your mind. But at that point, you are the most vulnerable to saying something you will regret.

Instead of immediate confrontation, give your brain some time to move past your angry thoughts to formulate a more calm and reasonable response. This takes conscious work on your part to slow things down. Sometimes it takes five minutes to cool down, other times hours or even a week or more. Take the time necessary to formulate a professional and calm response. You are in control when responding to someone's poor behavior or attack. Don't allow one bad act to cascade into another. You are the leader, respond like one.

Remember, being upset and angry is not an acceptable defense when you say things you shouldn't. When a complaint is filed and you find yourself in court because of poorly chosen words, no one will ultimately care about the reason why you said what you did. The damage remains.

I was on a conference call with one of our agency's attorneys and other members of our regional office to discuss an enforcement penalty against a company. Our attorney wanted to drop the case due to technicalities. During the conversation, this attorney began making unsubstantiated allegations against the work of our investigator who conducted the investigation. I knew the attorney was only disparaging the investigator's work to make his own job easier. As the attorney continued talking, I could feel the anger rising within me. I wanted to let this guy have it. I knew this investigator was an honorable person who did a thorough job. I was livid that this attorney was trying to smear our employee. Preparing a case for court takes hours of hard work and effort by the attorney. It's hard work, but that's his job!! Instead of spending hours preparing a case, I believed he just wanted to take the easy way out. I was ready to pounce and tell this attorney what I really thought of him and his pathetic tactic. But as I went to speak, I realized I was going to say things I would regret—and there would be many people to hear it. So I did what I've done so many times. I held my fire. But the matter wasn't over.

After the call ended, I took the time I needed to calm down and gather my thoughts. Maybe I was too quick to judge the attorney's intentions. Maybe he knew something I didn't. Still, I was bothered by his assessment of the investigator and I wanted to defend my employee. So the next day, I called the attorney. As professionally and calmly as possible, I told him I didn't appreciate his attacks against our investigator. And I provided the reasons why I felt it was uncalled for. Would you be surprised if I told you the attorney didn't argue with me and apologized? He told me he never intended to attack the investigator personally. And now that I was calm enough to discuss the situation, I could see things in a different light.

While the attorney and I eventually agreed to disagree on the issue at hand, we maintained our working relationship going forward. He never again attacked one of my investigators the way he did on that conference call. I call that a win. And I continued to work with him on other cases for which he did a great job defending our enforcement actions. And it was all because I held my fire and talked to him calmly about an issue that really bothered me.

I've come to appreciate the art of measuring my words. I can pick a fight with someone when I'm upset, or I can choose to calmly explain my view of the situation. I can hurt someone with my words or I can choose to heal. I can spread negativity or positivity. It's all a matter of the words I choose to say. Use words to your advantage as a leader. Choose those that will uplift and motivate those around you.

***

As I wrote previously, employees are always watching you. If you use four-letter words in the workplace, so will they. If you tell tasteless jokes, they will, too. And if you use words that belittle others, so will they. But, of course, the reverse is true, too. When you start measuring your words carefully, employees will follow your example. That's what leaders do. They set an example for others to emulate. Before you know it, you'll begin to see others choosing their words carefully to build up others.

When I first joined the federal government, I was trained on how to react when a member of the public lost their temper. Talk about essential skills for the job. People usually got angry at me when I visited their place of business to examine their trucking safety records. The explosions happened quickly, and once they started, there was no stopping. Managers and workers alike quickly lost control of their words as they vented all of their anger and frustration at the government. Which, in this situation, was me. They raised their voices, maybe cursed, and told me I was responsible for everything wrong in the world. To hear their displays of fury, it was like I became the human embodiment of evil. But I didn't take it personally. I knew their anger wasn't directed at me but at the institution I represented. Still, it was uncomfortable, to say the least.

During these encounters, I could've chosen to fight back, to defend myself and the government. I could have quoted them all of the federal statutes that demanded they comply with my review. I could have explained that my office could issue subpoenas to force them to report to me. I could have reminded them that if they so much as touched me I could have them shipped off to federal prison. I could have said and done many things—but I didn't. I did what I was trained to do in these situations. Nothing. I stood there and listened to them.

Obviously, there are limits to this, and I would not put up with verbal abuse. But I didn't strike back, even though I wanted to. I didn't engage them in their anger by shouting back at them. I held my fire. And after a few minutes, they got tired of venting and most cooperated fully with my review of their business.

Holding your fire when someone is verbally attacking you isn't easy. It's human nature to want to defend, strike back, and fight for your pride. Doing the exact opposite is incredibly difficult and takes a lot of discipline. A key strategy to stay calm and hold your fire is to think about the end goal. If I let angry business owners rile me up to the point of giving them a piece of my mind, they'll only dig their heels in more. And if I say something I should not, they are just waiting to report me to my agency. However angry I might be, I still need to do my job. Focusing on the task at hand can help you overcome the angry emotions you feel in the moment.

By holding my fire, I was able to stay in control of the situation. Angry people are just looking for a fight. They want you to engage with them so they can kick their tirade into high gear. But my lack of response and engagement threw them off. Such a response confuses them. It might make them more angry at first since you aren't giving in to their demands. But they'll begin to calm down, and once they do, they'll cooperate. Maybe just a little at first, then more as they realize they can't escape the situation no matter how they express their rage. It was amazing to watch. I said nothing but positive, calming words in response to the anger I received. I kept working toward my goal of getting the business to cooperate with my review. Even though I entered businesses with insults thrown at me on many occasions, I left shaking the hands of those same people many times.

I told you those stories because just like the companies I had to review, you will get employees that attempt to stir up your anger. You will have employees that try to get you to say something you should not. You will have employees that lose their temper and want you to do the same. Don't fall for it. You can't win that game. Don't play it with them. Don't lose your cool, don't resort to insults, and don't strike back. Measure your words, stay calm and address the situation. And don't let your ego get in the way.

Remember, as the leader you usually hold all the cards. You are the supervisor. You will have the last word. You hold the power. You don't have to yell. Even in the government, I had the power to give people weeks off without pay. I had the power to rate them as unsatisfactory. I had the power to promote and terminate. And I did. Don't let the little stuff get under your skin. Your calm, professional response will show everyone that you are a leader.

When you find yourself facing an angry tirade from a colleague, client, or employee, remember to stay calm, control your tongue, and project confidence. Keep your emotions under control in order to work your way through the issue. That's what a true leader does.

I began this chapter with a proverb about how it's easier to take a city than control one's tongue. And I could restate that proverb another way to say that it takes more courage, dedication, and strength to control one's tongue than it does to conquer a city. It's difficult, but you can do it—I know you can. Hold your fire, measure your words, and be the example your employees need to see. This might be one of the best disciplines you will ever build into your professional—and personal—life. And the best part? You can start right here, right now.

Now you are ready to learn about something that we all want and desire. No, it's not money, but it's close. It's a natural thing, it's a human thing. Many would say it's a good thing. But as a leader, you need to keep this desire in check because it will sink you just as fast as a loose tongue.

Chapter 21
Lessons in Self-Control
Key Takeaways and Applied Knowledge

Take it Further: Take a selfie on this topic, write down what you see? How would you rate your level of self-control? What steps do you need to take to improve in this area?

Chapter 22

SHE LIKES ME NOT

Lessons in Perceived Popularity

I had to do it. I was the designated bad guy. My wife and I discussed it. We debated it. We went back and forth on it for hours, discussing the pros and cons. Now it was final. A decision was reached. And I was the one who had to convey the message. It was a "no" message to my daughter's wish. It was not going to be easy. I wanted my kids to like me. As a dad I craved their love and affection. I loved to say "yes" to their requests. So I hated to do this. It was all so unfair that I was the one, the unlucky one who had to give the message. This was going to permanently hurt my daughter, I thought, and she was never going to forgive me. But it had to be done. I had to tell her "no."

It would be years, I thought, until she would speak to me again. Life is just not fair. And so I said "no" to her request and explained the reasons behind it. It did not go well. And as far as her forgiving me and my wife, well it's taken a bit longer than we anticipated. Like seventeen years and counting. But we're good. And oh, what was the request that I had to give her the bad news on, you ask? She wanted a cat.

Everyone wants to be liked by others—it's a hallmark of humanity. It isn't a bad thing. We all have our own ways of being social and forging relationships with others. Sometimes, to be liked, we put up with things we don't like all that much. Have you ever been out with a group of friends and they want to get dinner at that restaurant you're not crazy about? Since they're your friends and you want to spend time with them, you go along with it anyway. We do similar things for our kids, spouses, parents—you name it. When I was growing up, there was a song called "The Things We Do for Love." We do things we might not like because we love the people in our lives and we want them to be happy with us. We want to stay in the good graces of the people we care about.

But in the workplace, wanting to be liked and loved can become a dangerous trap when you're a supervisor. Just like every other relationship we have, we give in to things we're not crazy about just to remain likable and popular. Your employees may like you. They may say nice things about you and tell everyone what a wonderful boss you are. That's great, right? But let's say you notice their performance level is dropping and you start to find issues with the quality of their work. When you're desperate for their approval, it's difficult to confront employees about this. I heard about a supervisor who was in this exact position. He knew his employees' work quality wasn't as good as it should have been, but he let it go. He overlooked the problem because, as he put it, "Well, they like me and I don't want to be a jerk."

This desire to be liked can exert even more pressure when one is promoted to supervise the same peers, friends, and colleagues they worked alongside. You want to believe you're still one of the group. You may have social relationships that continue with colleagues even though you now supervise them. It becomes difficult to escape the pull of friendships that were established over years of working together as peers. And as a new supervisor, you still want to maintain those work friendships. You want to be liked by the group you now supervise. As issues surface and problems arise that require fair supervision, it's easy to be torn between old friendships and the responsibilities of the new job.

> *"This desire to be liked can exert even more pressure when one is promoted to supervise the same peers, friends, and colleagues they worked alongside. You want to believe you're still one of the group."*

Make no mistake: placing the desire to be liked in the workplace over obtaining results will result in failure every time. Desiring what is best for the business—for efficiency, quality assurance or profits—must be above the desire to be liked or popular. Chasing after likes and acceptance is fine in your personal life but not in the professional world.

As a leader, you owe it to your organization to get results first and foremost. And in the end you will not be judged on how well-liked you were. It's a nice thing to say someone was liked by their employees. I hope my employees feel that I was a good person and a fair leader to them. There is nothing wrong with that. This is about putting things into perspective, and being liked is not the primary goal.

And let's get real here: if you are doing your job and leading as you should, there will always be someone who is unhappy with your decisions. It's guaranteed, so get over it. Every decision you make is not going to be popular, that is a certainty. "You cannot please everyone" is a saying that is very true. And if you try you will sacrifice results and in the end hurt yourself and your employees.

***

You must be willing to make unpopular decisions as a leader. Actually, let me clarify. If you want to succeed as a leader, you must make unpopular decisions. Decisions where not all of your employees will be clapping and cheering for you. Decisions that are correct and necessary but unpopular nonetheless. I've had to enforce decisions like these numerous times throughout my career. Why? Because it was the right choice for my employer. Employees have pressed me time and time again about the production goals I set for them. "Can't they be lower?" they asked me. "These are difficult to reach," they said. My reply was courteous but firm: No, I'm not changing the goals because they are entirely within reach. This certainly is not what all my employees wanted to hear. Telling them there are standards and that they are expected to meet those standards is not exactly fun. It definitely doesn't help you make friends or be liked by everyone. Yet there is no escaping this responsibility that comes with being a leader.

Moving to a new office in the government was always a recipe for an unpopular decision causing someone to take offense at the location of their new workspace. In 2020, I was responsible for working with the designers of our new office space. I made tough decisions, based on the available space, as to where everyone would be located. Some got closer to windows, others did not. Some had offices, others did not. I gathered input from my employees, asked them their opinions and I kept them in the loop as to what was happening. But in the end, I had to make tough choices and finally an unpopular decision.

From experience, I knew someone would not like their new workspace. Sure enough, when the first sketch of the new design was given to employees, one took offense. He came into my office and began making his case as to why his space needed to be moved. And he told me exactly where he thought it belonged. I liked this employee, he did a good job. But he did not understand the limitations of designing an office. You can't just move one spot without moving something else. I listened to him and then told him, "No, I'm not moving it." I explained my reasons, and was nice about it, but that was the end of it. He was not happy, but he got over it. It was the right decision. And the new space turned out beautiful.

If there is one piece of advice that I have found to be very true it's that you will never please everyone. You won't; and don't try. Your job is to get results first and do the best you can to keep employees happy if possible. I can't look at every decision with the fear that it may be unpopular with someone. That's not how you lead. Of course, you try to keep folks happy. It would be easy to be a leader if every decision you made was about happiness. But it's not. Happiness is not always your number one goal.

Sometimes you really want to say "yes" to a request, but wisdom tells you otherwise. When I worked for the federal government in California, my agency signed a cooperative agreement with a State of California agency. This agency enforced similar regulations as my agency did in the area of transportation of household goods. The agreement stipulated that they would assist us by investigating some of our complaints and we would provide them with access to our national database. Both sides benefited. The state agency desperately needed the data we possessed, and we were happy to provide it. Our relationship started out well until a supervisor with this agency asked if I could do her a favor. She asked for a generic letter, with my signature on it, that her employees could use whenever they encountered opposition from a company her agency needed to investigate. It was sort of a right-of-entry request. My agency letterhead and my name would help her employees obtain cooperation. This was not in the agreement we signed.

But I told her I would think about it and I did. I wanted to say "yes." I wanted to please my new state partner. I gave it much thought and then declined. I explained my reasons: first, it was the state agency's responsibility to get the right of entry to a company's records. I could not become the primary method her employees used to get access to records. Her agency had to do that. Second, I did not want to provide my name and signature as a blank check that, once given, could never be taken back. They could use it for years, even after I was gone. And they could use it whenever they wanted. I had to say "no."

But then I offered her a compromise. I told her that my office would be willing to help her agency deal with uncooperative companies, but not in the way she asked. This way, I had more control over how my name and agency were being used.

But the state supervisor was unhappy with my offer. She stopped responding to emails and became upset with my office. The level of cooperation from her agency dropped significantly for a while. It was a tough decision, but it was the right one. I was disappointed in her response, but I knew I made the right call. In the end, she came around and our relationship improved.

Sometimes tough decisions aren't even up to you. They are decided by superiors above you and it's your job to carry them out.

The most unpopular decision my agency ever made was prohibiting employees from taking government vehicles home at the end of the workday. Employees were permitted to park their government vehicles at home and only use them when they went directly to their assignment in the field. This saved them a lot of time from taking the cars into the city, where our offices were located, and parking them at the start and end of each day. With the change in policy, this all ceased. Instead of heading home after their last assignment in the field, employees now had to drive back to the office and park the government car. I heard more gripes and complaints about this policy than any other one I had to enforce. A lower-level supervisor came to me and asked if our office could bend the rules a little bit. "Employees have taken these vehicles home for years," he explained. "They've come to expect it, so let's be reasonable." And since the rule itself came from the Washington, D.C., office, nobody would see the government vehicles missing from our California garage, right?

A leader makes decisions based on facts, not popularity. Contrary to what some employees may think, I don't go out of my way to make their lives more difficult. I listen to what my employees think and what they have to say. I try to make their jobs better and more productive for everyone. But at the end of the day, it's my job to enforce the agency's policies. I'm not paid based on how popular I am with my employees. I'm paid to implement the agency's orders. And I'm responsible for making sure everyone follows policy and achieves results. And as I've covered in an earlier chapter, if you don't get results then you'll soon find yourself looking for another job. The more you consider being liked in the decisions you make, the more susceptible you are to making bad decisions that will come back to bite you.

As much as I wanted to keep letting employees take government vehicles home at the end of the workday, I had to follow the agency's directive. What if someone got in a car accident driving one of the vehicles home when it was supposed to be in the office parking lot? I didn't want to be on the hook for that. So I explained to the supervisor that we had to follow the new policy. To assuage any employee anger, I agreed to speak with upper management when I had the chance and ask them to reconsider their decision. And I took every chance I got to do just that. But in the meantime, I held my ground and enforced the policy in spite of its unpopularity. It was the right thing to do.

Now, I didn't like doing this. I didn't want to make things more difficult for my employees. But making tough, unpopular decisions is part of the job. When you make decisions based on wanting to be liked by others, get ready to be rolled over and stepped on. Employees will take advantage of the fact that you want to be popular with them. They will push, relax, and bend the rules to no end—just as it happens with friends, spouses, and children. But remember: what is okay in our personal lives doesn't work in our professional lives. Once you give in to a request—like a supervisor asking me to let employees take government cars home—you better be prepared to give in again and again and again.

Thankfully, there's good news in all of this. There is a better way to handle the desire to be liked by your employees and others: seek to be respected more than liked.

Employees respect a supervisor for competency, fairness, and their ability to hold people accountable. And news flash: you can hold employees accountable and produce results without being a jerk. My employees know that I'm about the job—that's my main focus. And I make decisions based on what's best, not what's most popular that day. If I notice quality issues with our work, I address them. If I notice an employee is not performing to full potential, I talk to them privately about it. If employees, even the best ones whom I rely on daily, begin taking long lunches, I discuss it with them. I don't let things slide so people will like me. By treating everyone fairly and applying office standards to everyone equally, I earn respect from them. As you begin to live this out in your workplace, you will start to see that even though employees may disagree with you at times, they respect you as a leader. They know that you are putting your responsibilities above popularity.

I've found in my career that people respect a leader who makes tough decisions. People respect a leader who hears them out and listens. People respect a leader who achieves success, and they want to learn how to realize that same success. People respect a leader who holds them accountable. People respect a leader who raises the bar and upholds high standards. People respect a leader who has the courage to say "no." People respect a leader who is not striving to be the most popular. People respect a leader whose principles don't waver over time.

You earn people's respect by doing the right thing. You earn it by making thoughtful, business-focused decisions. You earn it by listening to employees and trying when you can to address their concerns. You earn it by communicating and being open about why you made certain decisions. When others respect you as a leader then other benefits will follow. And dare I say that one of those benefits might, maybe, could be, that you will be more liked as a leader.

You don't need to seek popularity to be successful. When you do your job well, and make decisions based on results, you will earn respect. And in the workplace, respect is more important than popularity, anyway.

The desire to be well-liked by employees challenges even the best of leaders. It's something every leader struggles with from time to time. Oftentimes we like and appreciate the employees we work with, and we want them to like us in return. But the desire to be popular becomes a snare if it isn't controlled. Avoid this popularity trap by putting your job first. You may not always be liked but you will be well-respected—and besides, that's your ultimate goal.

Chapter 22
Lessons in Perceived Popularity
Key Takeaways and Applied Knowledge

Take it Further: Reflect on the key takeaways from this chapter and jot down your thoughts. Have you let personal popularity interfere with your decisions? If so, what steps will you take to change?

Chapter 23

FLY THE AIRPLANE

Lessons in Traps and Distractions

I was lined up on the runway ready for takeoff. I had just finished my pre-takeoff checklist, and announced my departure over the radio: *"This is Cessna 68762 departing runway 21 Johnson County."* I lined up in the center of the runway as I had been taught, pushed the throttle, and started full speed ahead. Keeping the plane centered in the middle of the runway, I zoomed along until reaching sixty knots—takeoff speed. Gently, I pulled the yoke back for a smooth liftoff. It was perfect. Climbing at 500 feet per minute, I took a moment to pride myself on a great liftoff. But then I heard it … a noise, coming from the passenger side, even though I didn't have any passengers. Loud and clear, it was a sharp banging noise. Whatever it was, it was a noise I definitely didn't want to hear when I was hundreds of feet off of the ground.

I glanced over to the passenger side of the cockpit and quickly recognized the problem—the passenger door was unlatched! *How did that happen!? What do I do now?!* I thought frantically. As I reached across the cockpit to try to close the door, an alarm went off in my head. *Stop!!! Remember what your flight instructor taught you!* As the door kept banging sharply, I realized I was being dangerously distracted. Here I was, trying to watch my cockpit dials, climb altitude, and speed all while trying to close the passenger side door. I heard my instructor's voice in my head: *Stop and fly the airplane.* So I did exactly what I was taught to do. I turned back toward the airport, landed the plane, and properly shut the door. Letting such a simple mistake distract me from flying the plane could have resulted in disaster, and for many pilots it has.

Distraction can similarly be disastrous for leaders, and it often brings the same bad consequences if not handled correctly. Leading is a lot like flying an airplane—there are many things clamoring for your attention. Meeting clients, handling company budgets, overseeing projects, the responsibilities are seemingly endless. And, unfortunately, so are the things capable of distracting us.

A poorly performing employee is one of the biggest distractions that can pull us away from the work we should be doing. Now those of you who work in the private sector don't have as much of an issue with this as those who work in the public sector. In the public sector it's much more difficult to fire someone who is not doing their job. There are a lot of steps involved—documentation, tracking, hearings, time for appeal … you get the picture. Like the open door banging on the plane, it's easy to put all of your focus on that one employee who isn't doing their job … until all of a sudden, you realize you aren't flying the plane any longer.

"A poorly performing employee is one of the biggest distractions that can pull us away from the work we should be doing."

If you find yourself in one of these situations, it's imperative to compartmentalize the problem. Just like ships have sealed compartments to isolate flooding and stay afloat, you must deal with the problem while staying on track and managing your responsibilities. It's tempting to put all of your focus and energy into "fixing" a problem employee. But keep things in perspective. If you have ten employees and nine of the ten are doing well, then your focus should be on the nine, not the one. The one employee causing trouble needs to be addressed, of course, but the other nine still need your leadership, too.

I knew a supervisor named Sue who learned this lesson the hard way. There was one employee in her office who turned other employees against her leadership. So she went to war with the disgruntled employees, nitpicking their work, their time, everything. Sue micromanaged these employees so much that she became consumed with it. And the more she focused on those difficult employees, the more the rest of her team lacked guidance and leadership, and their results suffered because of it. To make matters worse, Sue lost her temper on a few occasions and said things to her employees she definitely shouldn't have (remember how important it is to control your tongue?

Hold Your Fire!). Complaints were filed against her, and suddenly, Sue found herself on the defensive.

Obsessing over disgruntled employees like this causes you to lose sight of the bigger picture. Sue was so consumed by combatting employees who didn't like her that she forgot about the employees in the office who were trying to support her. Without effective leadership at the helm, Sue's office descended into chaos. And when turmoil constantly reins in an office the first place to look is the supervisor. The good employees in the office lost confidence in their leader and she was eventually re-assigned to another position. And the employees who caused her all of this grief remained employed.

Sue failed to do the most basic thing one must do as a leader. Instead of flying the plane, she got distracted and crashed it. Resist the temptation to become so focused on attacking, responding, tracking, emailing, and arguing with employees causing you problems that you forget to *lead*.

A few years after Sue left, I was promoted as the new supervisor in the same office. I inherited a few of her former foes. But I had a different strategy for handling these employees, one that would result in success rather than failure.

I knew going into my new promotion that I couldn't allow the reputation of Sue's former foes to be my main focus. Yes, I had to deal with them, but I also had other employees to manage. I was committed to being fair but firm with everyone. Before long, I had most of the good employees moving in step with me, supporting my leadership and achieving fantastic results for the office in the process. By making these employees my main focus, I gave them what they needed most to succeed—effective leadership. Investing my time, energy, and focus on hardworking employees ultimately made them even better achievers.

I did not neglect the employees who caused Sue so much grief. I was firm but fair with them. I held them accountable for their results just like everyone else. While I refused to compromise on big things such as production outputs, I was careful not to nitpick them. I sensed they were decent people who got off-track and needed good leadership to bring out their best. I gave them room to grow and showed I had confidence in their abilities. In my conversations with them, I brought their attention back to the basics of their job. I needed them to see why their work was important and how they played a vital role in helping our office reach our goals.

"Change doesn't happen overnight, of course. But it will happen eventually."

Change doesn't happen overnight, of course. But it will happen eventually. As I settled into my new promotion, I saw the impact of my strategy. It was succeeding with everyone. In fact, two of Sue's former foes later became some of my best performers in the office. One of them became a top producer for a number of years, and the other was my right-hand person for a long time.

Dealing with troublesome employees is inevitable. It's part of the job of being a leader. But don't make them the focus of your daily work. Avoid falling into the trap of obsessing over small inconsequential arguments. Keep your job and all of its responsibilities front and center. Above all else, remember to fly the plane.

***

Troublesome employees aren't the only distractions that prevent you from flying the plane. Just as fires are one of the most dangerous things that can occur in an airplane, so too are fires at work—urgent situations that require your immediate attention—and can be just as devastating. You planned your day and everything is going well when all of a sudden a fire breaks out. The rest of your day is spent on damage control, picking up the pieces of the mess and forging a path forward. And needless to say, nothing you had planned on accomplishing that day happened.

These office emergencies could be any number of things. In my line of work, fires could be caused by a congressional office calling to complain about the way one of their constituents was treated by my employees. Such a call prompts a frenzy of activity—emails flood my in-box, and everyone calls one another wanting to know what happened and how to respond. When a member of Congress got involved, so did many others in my agency. Sometimes the issue was elevated as high as the secretary of transportation. These types of fires could last for days and were incredibly distracting to the day-to-day work required to maintain results.

Fighting fires like this is necessary in every leadership position, regardless of your job or industry. Where I live in northern California, fires are a part of life during the summer and fall. And sometimes it seems like the entire state is on fire. The same is true in the workplace. Sometimes you may feel like your entire job is spent putting out fires. So how do you effectively stop them so you can focus on what really matters—achieving results?

When I started my new job as the division administrator of California, we had significant problems with bus crashes. Every few weeks there would be a bus incident or crash that required my office to go into firefighter mode. Truck crashes were bad enough, but bus crashes were always worse. Many times they were carrying passengers, and the tragedy often made headline news. More than a few times the National Transportation Safety Board got involved, which was a big deal for my office. These bus crashes were happening so frequently that they became a big distraction for my team. We couldn't work on anything else while dealing with the aftermath of so many crashes. Bus safety was part of our mission, but something here was failing. We were going in the wrong direction, and something had to change.

Fires leave destruction in their wake even when they are handled properly. If you're experiencing frequent fires like I was, then you need to start partaking in some fire-prevention activities. California conducts controlled burns and thins forests to help prevent fires, and local governments often bring in goat herds to eat down brush that could easily spark a fire. These officials identify problems that caused past fires and try to prevent them from happening through targeted mitigation and prevention activities. It's much safer—not to mention cheaper and more efficient—to prevent a fire from starting than to extinguish one.

> *"Fires leave destruction in their wake even when they are handled properly. If you're experiencing frequent fires like I was, then you need to start partaking in some fire-prevention activities."*

I knew my office needed to start taking preventative measures to prevent bus crashes. But before this could happen, I needed to identify the root of the problem. After poring over bus crash data with my office supervisors, we determined that our office's current bus enforcement activities were insufficient to prevent crashes. Our ongoing actions weren't making enough of a difference to have an impact. So I decided to commit more resources to enforcement activities on buses.

Working with my team we trained four employees whose job was focused solely on conducting bus investigations. I then worked with my office supervisors to assign inspectors to conduct bus inspections at casinos, parks, and other public places. The goal was to catch buses in operation to check their tires, brakes, and other vehicle-related items. We also did more on-site investigations at their main office, where we checked their paperwork, hours of service, and maintenance programs. These changes increased our number of bus investigations substantially.

Within one year the fires we had been dealing with constantly began to subside and then began to decrease as our program got underway. We continued this program for many years and found that it continued to reduce the number and severity of bus crashes in the state. Our prevention activities worked. We put out a forest fire and ensured we wouldn't have any others that size again. More importantly, lives were saved as a result of our efforts.

When you're constantly battling fire after fire, it is imperative that you take the time to address the root cause of the problems. Hard as you might try, you can't be successful staying in firefighter mode all the time. It drags you down mentally, steals your time, robs you of achieving crucial results, and can damage not only your career but your health, too. You can't fly the plane if you are continually distracted by new fires that demand your energy and resources.

One of the most dangerous aspects of battling fires in the workplace is that they cause a spiraling effect. As you battle more of them, you have less time to conduct the preventative work necessary to stop them. And the less preventative work you do, the more these fires happen, and the ugly cycle continues. If you find yourself in one of these spirals, it's time to take a step back and assess the situation. Work toward a change that will stop the spiral and commit to it. Don't stay in the spiral, it's called a death spiral in aviation for a reason – it only goes down.

If you have too many fires at work right now then take the time to analyze what is causing them. Fires usually don't start on their own, something ignites them. Find out what it is and then you can begin to deal with it. Go to the root of the problem and begin to address it. Start doing some preventative maintenance to reduce the likelihood of fire eruption. This takes more time and effort initially, but as you begin to address the real issue your time will come back to you. You are implementing a course of action for future fire prevention, which will pay off.

Keep at it as fires are not easy to extinguish completely, as we know here in California. They flare up again even after you thought they were out. Stay with it, don't quit, be persistent. As your problem fires die down your joy and job satisfaction will improve. You will have more time to visit clients, improve your business and spend your time in areas that help you succeed and thrive. And life at work will be much more pleasant for all involved.

Now, undertaking prevention work doesn't mean you'll never experience fires again. But it does mean that when fires do break out, the prevention work you did will go a long way in limiting their damaging impact.

***

On the opposite side of the distraction spectrum are nonsense items I like to call time wasters. These are the endless things that come up during the day that steal your time and shift your focus to unimportant things that ultimately don't matter. Whether it's phone calls, false alarms, or emails clogging up your inbox, these time wasters can distract you from flying the plane just as effectively as fires. But unlike fires, time wasters lack the same sense of urgency. If a coworker wants to call you and talk for an hour, you don't have to answer the phone. If your buddies want to go and spend half an hour each morning getting Starbucks, you don't have to go with them. These things are nice to do, but they aren't crucial to your job. And when you're in a management position, sometimes you'll have to limit your participation so you can get your work done.

Requests for assistance, while good, can also become a distraction. I supervised a large program and therefore was constantly being asked by other offices to review, contribute, or have my employees help with something that didn't directly affect my work. Notice I said "my" work. That meant work that was not in my performance plan or that of my employees. Basically, it's charity work. I tried to contribute when my peers and other offices asked, but such requests became a distraction that prevented me from working on my own tasks. For example, I was frequently asked to provide my employees to assist in training others. I liked helping, I liked giving my employees other opportunities. But I still had my job to get done. And at the end of the year, these other tasks did not count toward my investigation quotas. I was judged on what I accomplished. I still contributed but at times had to put limits on it. So I learned the art of saying "no." On the occasions when I did agree to assist, I kept the commitment narrow and short-lived. This is life as a leader. While you might want to help out every time someone asks, you have a job to do and you can't get it done when others are continually asking for your resources and time.

There are so many more distractions that can keep you from producing results. Employees and supervisors themselves can get distracted on what it is they need to be doing. They can go off on tangents, get stuck in the mud, and as a result fail to accomplish the work that the organization needs them to do. In my line of government work, employees were charged with enforcing civil codes, not criminal laws. And yet I can't tell you how many times I had to talk with employees, pull them out of the weeds, and set them back on track by refocusing them on the important tasks of their job.

And then there are false alarms—when someone sends you an email and tries to make it seem like it's incredibly urgent and you need to drop everything to handle it. Be careful not to fall into the trap of replying to everyone and trying to resolve every single problem as soon as possible. It's a recipe for burnout. Prioritize requests that come in according to their importance and urgency. If you know something doesn't have to be addressed the second it pops into your inbox, it can wait.

Fires, troubled employees, outside requests and unimportant items will all clamor for your attention as a leader. Keep your focus and energy on the things that produce the great results every leader needs to succeed. Invest your time in the activities that pay dividends in your work. And when distractions do arise, as they absolutely will, use good judgment on how and when to address them so you can keep doing what matters most: flying the airplane.

Chapter 23
Lessons in Traps and Distractions
Key Takeaways and Applied Knowledge

Take it Further: Identify your top distractions and how you can minimize their impact on your goals.

Chapter 24

TOSS THE ANCHOR

Lessons in Anchoring Bias

I'm a person who loves to tour ships, whether they be old battleships, aircraft carriers or even passenger ships. I'm amazed at the mechanical designs and the complexity of these crafts. I marvel at the enormous size and the engineering that it took to make them. Two of my favorite tours have been the battleship *North Carolina* and the aircraft carrier *Midway*. Walking through these ships was like going back in time. I could picture what it must have been like to be at sea on one of these crafts as it was firing its guns or launching aircraft. I walked the flight deck on the carrier *Midway* and could picture myself in a jet ready to get launched into the air. It was sobering looking at the big guns of the *North Carolina* and realizing these were actually fired in combat at our enemies in World War II.

What also stands out to me about these vessels is the anchors on them. I did not realize how big and massive the anchors are on these ships. They look small compared to the overall size of the ship, but when you get next to them, they are huge. Weighing thousands of pounds, they are held up by enormous chains operated by large machines. The anchor is large and heavy for a reason—it has to hold the ship in place. When the captain of a ship wants to restrict its movement, he drops anchor. And when the anchor is in place, it binds the ship to a small travel radius so it can't drift due to wind or current. They have one job and that is to restrict the movement of the ship when they are deployed. If the anchor is set correctly, the ship is not going anywhere. They are so simple yet so effective in what they do. Anchors are good for ships—they help protect them and keep them safe. But anchors are not good for you and me.

In fact there is a phenomenon called the anchoring bias which can be harmful to you as a leader. The bad thing is you may not realize it's being used. But it gets worse. Other people will throw these on you. And just like a ship, this anchor is going to bind you. And it will encourage you to make bad decisions. So let's take a closer look at this bias.

The anchoring bias occurs when you are presented with an initial piece of information and then make subsequent decisions based on that piece of information. In a classic example of this bias, study participants were told to think of the last two digits of their Social Security Number (SSN).[1] Once they had their SSN in mind, the participants were asked to estimate the cost of products such as wine or a cordless mouse. The study found that participants with higher SSNs guessed higher on the value of the products, while those with lower numbers estimated lower product values. The first number the participants

1   Dan Areily, *Predictably Irrational: The Hidden Forces That Shape Our Decisions, Revised and Expanded Edition, 2010*

thought of—the last two digits of their SSN—impacted their subsequent judgment.

Just like a ship's anchor, the first piece of information you are given binds you in a smaller radius when it comes to further decision-making. Let's say you want to sell your car for $10,000. A tentative buyer approaches you and offers you $5,000 instead. Needless to say, you're insulted by the offer and tell the buyer you wouldn't dream of selling the car for so little. But whether you recognize it or not, an anchor has been set in your mind. Instead of negotiations revolving around $10,000, they now revolve around $5,000.

In negotiations like this, the first one to throw out an offer usually has the advantage since they set the anchor that the rest of the negotiation will center around. This frequently happens in salary negotiations. When the hiring manager throws out the first salary offer, you take that initial number and base your subsequent counter offers around it. It's like an anchor was thrown out to sea and you are tied to it. Your best bet is to lead with your ideal figure and make the company start negotiation from your offer.

We're all subject to psychological anchors. And truth be told, these anchors are all around us. As a leader, it is imperative to know when you are being anchored. In order to overcome the constraints being placed on your decision-making, you first must recognize them.

As a supervisor in my agency, I required each of my trucking investigators to accomplish around thirty investigations each year. That was the standard. An investigator once came into my office and told me that, in his experience, twenty-four investigations in a year were more appropriate than thirty. I immediately sensed that an anchor was being set in an attempt to lower the number of yearly investigations. I heard the employee out anyway, before responding that thirty-six investigations were actually possible and in fact had been completed by others in previous years. The employee wanted me to negotiate from the lower number he proposed, but because I was able to recognize the anchoring bias, I responded with an even higher number. I wanted the negotiations to center around my number, not his. And when faced with the prospect of completing even more investigations each year, the employee accepted that thirty sounded reasonable.

Employees, customers, and others are going to throw anchors at you and they may not even realize what they are doing. But you as the leader responsible for results should recognize when an anchor is being set on you. Usually, these anchors will cause you to think about reduced numbers, reduced goals, and reduced results. I had an employee who was very loyal to me and did outstanding work. But when confronted with a difficult situation with a state agency that was paid to conduct work under a grant for my office, he tried to set an anchor on me. The state was at twenty percent achievement toward a goal that was important to my agency. They needed to be above eighty-five percent. My employee, who had worked at the state agency and knew how it functioned, informed me that not much could be done to change it. He explained the internal workings of this state agency and why it would not be possible for them to exhibit much improvement on this goal. I was somewhat shocked he would say this. He was basically telling me it was as good as it was going to get. We needed to accept it. That was the reality. I quickly disagreed.

> *"Employees, customers, and others are going to throw anchors at you and they may not even realize what they are doing. But you as the leader responsible for results should recognize when an anchor is being set on you."*

I told him I believed that the state could improve in this area. I told him I had seen this issue with other states and was able to work with them to improve their results. I informed him this was not a done deal and that he needed to work on solving the problem that was keeping them from better results. The option of the state not making progress on the goal was not on the table. I then reminded him that other states had obtained the higher goal in this area, and so could ours.

My employee had already set an anchor in his mind that this could not be changed. He was convinced it was not possible. And when asked about it he tried to set the anchor on me. Instead of talking about eighty-five percent or higher, he wanted to set the anchor at twenty percent, give or take a little. I would not let our discussions on the matter revolve around the twenty percent marker. I threw another anchor, 100 percent. That's where we had to get them and it was very possible.

What amazed me about this example is that after our discussion he began to brainstorm ways to get the state to improve. The anchor he had set in his own mind, or someone set on him, began to drift. He began to re-think the issue. He came up with ideas on how to move the state forward. He then came to me and asked for my blessing on his proposal. I was happy to see he moved off his "this can't be improved" to "we can do this." And he persisted with the state for some time and was able to get them to address the issue. The result? The state's level of compliance with the goal exceeded eighty-five percent, and many times was at 100 percent (it could vary from month to month). But the progress only happened when I refused to be anchored and helped an employee remove his own anchor.

Remember, the anchoring bias occurs when you base your decision on an initial piece of information that was given to you by someone else. Then, cognitively, you get tied to that initial anchor even if you disagree with it. And just like a ship can't drift far from its anchor, neither can you escape the boundaries set by that first number or offer. It can be difficult to recognize that this is happening. But when you are in a leadership position, you must be able to identify when someone is trying to anchor you and respond appropriately.

Eva M. Krochow, Ph.D. from the University of Leicester suggests three strategies to counter the effects of an anchor.[2] First, recognize when an anchor is being set on you. Pay close attention to the numbers or offers others throw at you in meetings or conversations at work. They are likely trying to box you in and anchor you to their ideal number, much like my employee did with his request to lower investigation numbers. But once you know the anchor exists, you can be more careful in making decisions.

Second, slow down the decision-making process. Those who want to anchor you are hoping you will immediately engage in negotiating and make a decision based on the information they provide you. Don't accept something just because someone says it. Take time to research the matter yourself. Do your homework. When my employee approached me with the "more appropriate" number of yearly investigations, I knew from experience—and my own data—that his number was too low. And when

2   Eva M. Krochow, Ph.D. *"Outsmart the Anchoring Bias in Three Simple Steps."* Psychology Today, February 11, 2019. https://www.psychologytoday. com/us/blog/stretching-theory/201902/outsmart-the-anchoring-bias-in-three-simple-steps

another employee informed me that the state could not improve on a performance goal, I also knew that was not true. In both situations, my experience informed me that their initial pieces of information were inaccurate. In each case, I brought out additional information they had not considered.

Third, throw out your own anchor in response. And throw it out way past where it was thrown on you. Make another offer that is either much greater or much lower than the offer you've given—whichever one places you in the negotiating range that you want to be in. I refuse to let others base the discussion on the anchor that they want around my neck. Early in my career in the government, one of my coworkers was responsible for settling penalties issued to companies for non-compliance with the department's safety regulations. My coworker's job was to negotiate the final amount of the fine so it would be as close to the original penalty as possible. One time he was in negotiations over a penalty with an owner of a trucking company. The Department's penalty against the owner was a $9,000 fine. The owner countered with $6,000. "Well," my coworker said—who, mind you, is a former Marine and tough as nails—"that's well short of the fine, which is now at $12,000."

"Twelve thousand dollars!?" the owner replied. "The claim letter clearly states the fine is $9,000."

"You want to lower the fine by $3,000, and I want to raise it by $3,000," my coworker said. "Let's meet in the middle." The owner paid the full $9,000 fine.

My coworker sidestepped the anchor trying to be set on him by counterpunching the offer and raising rather than lowering the fine. And he threw his own anchor out that brought the negotiations back to where he wanted them.

***

The anchoring bias is harmful to leaders because it often leads to damaging compromises that result in lower goals and standards. And the worst part is that you might not even realize it's happening. While learning about the anchoring bias can help you develop the ability to recognize and avoid it, there's another type of anchor that is not so easily conquered: personal anchors. These are anchors that family, friends, coworkers, supervisors, and even you place on you, whether intentional or not. It's the thoughts that say you aren't good enough. The ones that say you can't get that job, be accepted into that school, or be promoted into that position. Personal anchors always tell you that you are not smart enough, capable enough, or talented enough to accomplish better things in your life. These anchors can be the most difficult to break, especially if they were set on you early in life. If you let them, they can destroy your hopes and your dreams.

I'll never forget when one of my supervisors told me early in my government career that I wouldn't make it as a supervisor. I was stunned. Why would he say that? I asked myself. He told me I wasn't aggressive enough to be a successful supervisor.

"You're too quiet," he told me.

This is a classic case of an extrovert thinking that introverts are not as capable as they are when it comes to leadership. They think a leader has to be forceful and order people around to get things done. It's a big mistake to think that way, but it's even worse to throw an anchor on someone else based on that mistaken philosophy. I told the supervisor I disagreed and left it at that. I didn't accept his statement as true. I knew I was more than capable of being a great leader in the workplace. I threw off his anchor and went on to prove him wrong throughout my more than thirty years of leadership in the government.

People will try to anchor you with harmful thinking that keeps you from reaching your full potential. No matter where you're at in life or what you are trying to accomplish, someone will try to anchor you down.

When my daughter was in college, she decided to pursue a Ph.D. in physics. Part of the grad school admittance process involved passing some challenging tests, which many students failed on their first attempt. After struggling on her first test attempt, one of the professors told her she may not have what it takes to get a Ph.D. She could have taken the professor's words to heart and quit. She could have let his anchor weigh her down and destroy her dreams. But she did the opposite and allowed the anchor to motivate her.

She informed the professor that she did not accept his statement. She reminded the professor of all her field accomplishments and excellent academic record. She told the professor she had the knowledge and abilities to be in the Ph.D. program. She threw off the anchor that was unfairly being set on her. She went on to successfully pass all of the grad school admittance requirements and graduated from one of the nation's top physics Ph.D. programs. The professor, who had initially questioned her abilities, was one of the first to congratulate her on her achievement.

What anchors have been placed on you? What are the limiting beliefs others have set on you that you need to shake off? Don't let others throw an anchor on your future, your career, and your success. Throw off every anchor that's holding you down and cast them back into the sea—where they belong.

Chapter 24
Lessons in Anchoring Bias
Key Takeaways and Applied Knowledge

Take it Further: Consider how the concepts in this chapter apply to your career or personal goals. What anchors have others set on you? What is holding you back? What anchor do you need to toss back into the sea?

Chapter 25

YOU HAVE THE BALL - RUN

Lessons in Taking the Initiative

In football, nothing is more comical than watching a simple kick play go afoul. It's fourth down, the team on offense has its kicking unit on the field. The punter is in the backfield ready to kick the ball. The ball is hiked to the kicker but it's not on target. The ball flies over the punter's head. The punter runs back and struggles to get the ball, only to realize he does not have enough time to kick it. The play is screwed up. The simple hike-and-kick-the-ball play is no more. The kicker stands holding the ball, looking like he's completely lost and in a state of shock. Looking as if he's waiting for someone to tell him what to do. Here is where the fun part starts.

Kickers are not trained to run the ball. Their job is to kick the ball. But here is the kicker, with the ball, but he can't kick it. So what's the next best thing to do—stand around and wait to be pummeled? No! Run! Run the ball! Thousands of remote fans are screaming at the TV—run! Don't you practice this?? I know that wasn't the plan but deal with reality. Run the ball. Do the best you can. It's not complicated, the job is to advance the ball as far as possible. But they don't, they run aimlessly around the backfield like they are lost as the defense of the other team pours on them like a swarm of bees. It usually ends badly.

Are you the type who likes to ask your boss for permission on what to do next at work? Do you always want direction from your superior? If so, then listen up. This behavior doesn't always fly when you become a leader yourself.

This topic never became more clear to me than when I attended a meeting with my fellow division administrators (DAs)—high-level field leaders in my agency—and superiors from agency headquarters. DAs are responsible for all agency operations in the respective states in which they work. It's sort of like commanding a ship at sea for the U.S. Navy. The DA steers the ship, runs the grant programs, oversees the investigations in their state, and is the supervisor for all of the agency's employees in the state. The DA calls the shots—according to agency guidelines, of course.

Every so often my agency would have a national meeting where all fifty DAs met together with senior leaders at headquarters. It was question-and-answer time at one of these meetings when one of the DAs asked a question I could hardly believe. In front of leaders from headquarters, who oversee millions of dollars of federal funds, thousands of employees, and set national guidance, one DA raised their hand and asked about the proper coding to use on an employee's timecard. Say what? Yes, a DA actually asked an executive leader of the agency a question about timecards.

It may have been a valid question. But not to an executive leader of the agency. The DA had other options available to them to get their question answered rather than asking it at a high-level meeting. Asking such a simplistic question brings your ability to lead into question. Judicious evaluation of the questions you ask of your supervisors is an integral aspect of leadership. I never ask my boss about items that, if I do my homework, I could solve on my own. She's busy—I don't want to take up her precious time with issues that I can find the answer to myself.

When should you ask your supervisor for assistance? In his book, Admiral Bull Halsey, author John Wukovits describes an incident with the admiral that could have doomed a fellow Navy captain's career. Admiral Halsey was a no-nonsense, go-get-the-enemy-type of person. One of his mottoes was "Shoot first, and we'll argue afterward." The admiral expected commanders to make their own on-the-spot decisions.

This particular captain under Halsey's command was in charge of an aircraft carrier and his planes were in the air as a storm approached. The captain was concerned that trying to land them in a rainstorm would result in disaster. Instead of making his own call on it he consulted with Admiral Halsey about what he should do. The captain's staff held their breath as they expected Halsey to explode at such a trivial question. The admiral calmly replied that he did not care and that if he wanted to go around the storm prior to landing the aircraft that was fine. But the captain then made a terrible mistake, he asked another question of the admiral. He asked whether he should turn right or left to go around the storm. Admiral Halsey, obviously annoyed, vowed to block any further promotion of the captain (fortunately for the captain, a promise he did not keep).[1]

I'll admit there is a fine line between asking your superior for guidance and figuring things out on your own. If you ask too many questions, they may think you aren't competent to lead in your position. But if there's a major decision to be made and you don't involve them, they may be unhappy if you forge ahead on your own and things end up failing. So how can you ever choose what's right?

I suggest you use knowledge of your supervisor and of the issue to guide you. Learn to sense when your supervisor wants to be involved with an issue and when they would rather you handle it. Then, tailor your questions based on similar problems you've worked on in the past. As you do this, you'll gain a better sense of how your supervisor wants you to handle things and how much involvement they desire. Of course, it takes time and effort, like everything else we've discussed so far. But it works. I've done this with every supervisor I've had. Each one has appreciated how I learned to handle issues and worked

---

1   Wukovits, *Admiral "Bull" Halsey,* p. 40

with them in a manner that made both of us grow and improve.

> *"Learn to sense when your supervisor wants to be involved with an issue and when they would rather you handle it."*

Now, you should not hesitate to ask for guidance when you truly need it. I've asked my supervisors for advice many times. But it usually revolved around bigger issues, major projects, and serious personnel issues. I've never asked them how to code a timecard or how to file certain paperwork. Other folks in our agency specialize in those areas whom I can ask. I would never bother my supervisors with such minor issues.

Before you ask your supervisor a question, check with yourself first: is there another way I can get an answer to this question? Did I do my proper research first before I bother someone else about it? Why am I asking my supervisor for help on this? Asking yourself these questions will help you determine if an issue you're facing does, in fact, require your supervisor's guidance or if there are other options available to you to solve the problem at hand.

If you determine that you need help from your supervisor regarding a matter, there are few best practices to follow that will set you up for success. Do your homework. Seek out all of the information you need to inform your supervisor about the issue. Next, provide a few options, each supported with facts, for how you could proceed on the matter. Let your supervisor know the option you'd like to move forward with and why. This shows that you have researched the matter and have taken the time to think things through. It also shows initiative that you are sharing your insight on the option that you think is the best. This allows for good discussion as you elicit their advice.

Contrast this with you throwing the issue to your supervisor, with few facts and documentation, and asking them to make the decision. You are asking them to do all the work. When one of my subordinates engaged me on an issue, one of my first questions was asking them for their opinion. What facts did they have, had they researched the topic, were other options available, and what were the pros and cons of each? I asked them clarifying questions to get all the facts and see if they did their homework. I frequently asked them, "Which do you think is the best way to proceed?" And when the subordinate had done their homework and gathered the facts, it allowed for productive and thoughtful conversations. I enjoyed having those conversations and working with them to make sound business decisions.

Don't make your supervisor do all the work. Instead, help them arrive at good decisions with you. Show initiative and don't be afraid to discuss options and give your opinion. Some may not like this method because it puts the burden of results on them instead of their supervisor. If it fails, they worry that they're on the hook for it. But this is not a leadership mentality. If you're going to run from the consequences of decision-making, you should not be in a leadership position. Leaders make decisions and they move forward.

Ultimately, your supervisor will determine whether to follow your lead or choose another option. And if they decide to go another route, that's fine, you still did your job. So don't let it bother you. If you follow this process ten times and you win seven of the ten, you're doing great. Be a partner in the decision-making process with your supervisor, not a bystander. Make the decision as easy as possible for your supervisor.

At the other end of the spectrum is a supervisor who wants to be involved in every little issue. It is frustrating to feel that you aren't trusted to make decisions yourself. If you find yourself in this situation, slowly show your supervisor that you are confident and competent to make decisions on your own. This is a process that may take some time. I remember a supervisor who told me how I should design a presentation I was tasked to give to senior leaders in my agency. I had been with the agency for over thirty years at that point. I'd given literally hundreds of presentations to leadership and industry. Yet he wanted to dictate to me how my presentation should look. A few of my peers were also giving presentations to the same senior leadership group. We all did a dry run for my supervisor so he knew what we would be presenting. Then he stated that he wanted mine to match the others. He wanted all of us to look the same.

I did not like it. I'm very picky about giving presentations. I like to be original, I like lots of visual aids, catchy charts and few words. And if I'm giving the presentation, I have to own it. I can't let someone tell me how to give "their" presentation. It won't work for me.

He asked our group if we agreed that our presentations would look similar to one another. I calmly spoke up in opposition. I explained our options for presenting and why being a little different from each other was okay. I told him I wanted to be part of the whole, but also show my uniqueness. That would get lost with all of our presentation designs looking the same. I offered to keep similar colors but wanted the freedom of design and style. He thought about it, he got quiet for about ten seconds. Then he said, "Okay, do it your way." I was relieved. And he did not regret that decision. My presentation was a huge success, praised by everyone in leadership. And my supervisor was the first one to send me a text afterward. It was short. He said, "Awesome Job!!"

On other occasions, I made similar suggestions, always leading my supervisor to let me handle things and trust my judgment. In time he began to trust me more and more. I knew I had arrived at where I wanted to be when his secretary called me about an important hiring issue. She said, "I spoke to Doug. He said, 'Do whatever Steve sees fit.'" It was an affirmation of my running the ball, handling decisions, and making good things happen. The more you do your homework, gather the facts, and offer ideas on how to address issues, the more you'll be noticed for your competent decision-making skills. Before you know it, you'll be hearing, "Don't worry about running that by me. Go ahead and proceed as you see fit." That's when you know you're doing it right.

***

Now, let's look at the other side of this question, how should you react when your employees come to you for assistance? Again, there is a way in which you can grow your employees through this process or impede their development. And it is in your best interest, as always, to make them grow.

As a supervisor, I want my subordinates to ask me questions. I want to be consulted on important matters and involved in issues that significantly impact our agency's goals. When someone is new to a position, I expect questions from them—that's normal. And during their onboarding period, I prioritize taking the time to train them and provide a solid foundation upon which they can succeed. But after they have been in their position for some time, I expect them to start learning how to solve problems independently.

Let me be clear here: I'm talking about solving routine day-to-day issues, not earthshaking decisions that will affect the entire organization. Simply put, I don't want to be flooded with emails about simple things that my employees should be able to handle. I want them to think through issues, solve problems, and lead. I prefer they take action and keep me informed only if necessary.

I gave my subordinate supervisors and employees authority and flexibility to make decisions on their own. When given the space to learn and make decisions, employees gain valuable experience problem-solving routine issues. And when bigger issues arise, they will be more confident and competent to address them based on their past experience. Eventually, your employees will reach the point where they won't need to rely on you as much to help them handle things. This makes your life as their supervisor much easier. Rather than being bombarded with questions about routine issues, you'll be able to concentrate on pressing tasks more effectively. And the best part? The space you give your employees to learn by doing enables them to become better leaders themselves. There's no longer a need to micromanage your employees because they can be trusted to make wise decisions on their own. And as your employees grow in ability, your results always improve. That's a win-win scenario.

If you have been placed in charge of a ship, then steer it. If you have the ball, run with it. Don't panic and ask which way to turn the ship or which direction to go. Instead, do what you know will work. Use the training you've received or search for new information when necessary. Save the questions for when you need guidance only your supervisor can provide. You've been placed in a leadership position for a reason—you have what it takes to lead. So run, lead and make good things happen.

Now I'm going to show you how to be visible to others. Maybe you feel like you've been invisible to leadership in your work. That's about to change. I'm going to show you how to make yourself appear. And you are going to look marvelous.

Chapter 25
Lessons in Taking the Initiative
Key Takeaways and Applied Knowledge

Take it Further: Challenge yourself to identify one area where you need to take the initiative.

Chapter 26

CAN YOU SEE ME NOW?

Lessons in Getting Noticed

It's what great careers are made of; starting at the bottom of the food chain and working your way up to the biggest and best-paying jobs at the company. And a huge part of getting to the top is getting those above you to notice you. If they don't know you are there, how can they promote you? If they don't hear or see much of you, how will you get noticed? In any organization, there are *lots* of people trying to get noticed as they vie for the top jobs. So how do you distinguish yourself from others? How do you get supervisors and executives to see your talent and promote you to greater things?

There are right ways and wrong ways to get noticed. Of course, you want to get noticed in the right ways because these are the most likely to result in a promotion. While the wrong ways *will* get you noticed, they're not exactly putting you on the path to success. I want to give you a few examples of how you can get noticed, but there's a catch: these methods I'm about to share with you can have both positive and negative consequences. They showcase both right and wrong ways to garner attention, so you need to be careful. I'll show you how to use each of them to your benefit.

The most prevalent complaint my government organization received on its employee feedback surveys was that promotions were not based on merit. In other words, people think it's who you know. Promotions are based on the level of friendship you enjoy with those in power, who you golf with on the weekends, or who you're having drinks with at happy hour. People think decisions on advancement are based on all of these external factors that are out of reach to many. In their view, what's the point of even trying? It's all a setup, anyway.

Now, I don't deny that these things happen. I've seen people get promoted for over thirty-five years in the military, in the private sector, and in government. Some of them got their promotion just because of who they knew. No matter how fortunate it may seem, being promoted solely based on connections eventually leads to failure. That's because promotions based on reasons other than the ability to lead and perform the job will always lead to problems and reduced results. Promoting someone because they are a "buddy" or a member of the "in" crowd is not a results-based selection. And catapulting someone who is unprepared for leadership is not smart or healthy for the organization in the long run.

While promotions based on connections do occur, it's a mistake to think that this is the right way to get noticed or even that most people get promoted this way. I've seen many, many more people throughout the years who earned their promotions based on their talent and success alone. So, let me give you a few tips on how to get noticed the right way in your career. Remember what I said before—these suggestions can either help or hurt you. Ready to get started?

"While promotions based on connections do occur, it's a mistake to think that this is the right way to get noticed or even that most people get promoted this way."

The first rule to getting noticed the right way is to be positive. There are always complainers in any organization—you know the type. They gripe about the work they have to do, their supervisor, lack of resources, or any number of external factors as to why they can't do their job. They would be better, but they complain they don't have enough training. They could do the work, but say their supervisor is too constricting. They could get better results, if people would just cooperate with them. You see the pattern here. Whenever someone like this encounters a problem, they blame others for it. This gets you noticed for all of the wrong reasons. And it brings failure to your doorstep.

But as I'm sure you know all too well, complaining is easy to do. I've been guilty of it. And once you start complaining it's difficult to stop. Before you know it, you're not even thinking of solving the problems you're complaining about, you're just complaining about anything and everything. No one wants to promote a complainer. Not only is their negativity contagious, but they have no problem-solving skills to speak of. I've seen many capable employees throughout my career who could have been much more successful had they not been chronic complainers.

> *"Once you're known as a complainer, you aren't going anywhere in the organization. It will kill your career."*

Complaining is not a healthy practice, so change the pattern. For example, if there is a communication problem between you and other employees, help resolve it instead of griping about it. Use the energy you would've spent complaining and redirect it into working as hard as you can to solve the problem. Supervisors want to promote employees who have a positive attitude and who know how to problem-solve. Complainers are a dime a dozen, you'll find them in droves. But leaders find ways, invent ways, make ways to succeed. They don't let external factors stop them. They push forward, and in the process, they get noticed.

If you don't take the initiative to be part of the solution instead of the problem in your workplace, then you don't belong in a leadership position. And if you find yourself in a job where you just cannot stop complaining, then do something else. For your own health and career prospects, find another career that will benefit you and the employer. Seek out an organization where you can be positive, happy, and productive. It's never too late to change. You might be a complainer today, but that doesn't mean you must be one tomorrow. If you want to be a leader and be considered for promotions, cultivate the positive, can-do attitude hiring managers always seek.

There was a popular song back in 1974 called "Billy Don't Be A Hero," about a union soldier who goes off to war. Before he left, his fiancée told him, "Billy, don't be a hero, come back and make me your wife." Later on in the song, when the battle is raging, the army sergeant cries out that he needs a volunteer to ride out and bring back some extra troops. Billy's hand goes up, forgetting everything his fiancée told him about not being a hero. Well, as I'm sure you've guessed by now, the song doesn't have a happy ending. Billy doesn't come back from war, and when his fiancée receives a letter in the mail telling her what a hero Billy was, she throws it away.

While volunteering was a high-risk venture for Billy, it's required for the rest of us if we want to get noticed for bigger and better things in the workplace.

Volunteering isn't always easy. If it was, everyone would do it. It's extra work—not to mention extra stress—on top of everything else you're expected to do. But despite the additional workload, volunteering provided me with opportunities to grow professionally and opened up avenues to promotion. I joined volunteer teams at work and soon before I knew it, I was giving presentations to top executives in my agency. My involvement in these projects resulted in invitations to volunteer for other projects that again gave me the opportunity to be around upper management. This is how you get noticed. This is how you build a resume. And as these volunteer projects succeeded, supervisors equated those results to me.

By solving problems and achieving results through volunteer work, I was proving to those above me that I had great potential to be successful in higher positions of authority and leadership. So of course, every time I was asked to volunteer at work I said yes! And let me say, not every project I volunteered for was glamorous. On a number of occasions, I was asked to train new employees. It was really a thankless job, with lots of responsibility and could be as long as a one-year commitment. I said yes each time I was asked. I stepped up and did it for my supervisor. They appreciated my willingness to help them and in return, they volunteered me for greater opportunities.

Eventually, I was asked to be on regional and national teams where I received more exposure. Looking back over the course of my career, I realized how much visibility I received from my work on these groups. I received many awards and recognitions for my participation and I developed a reputation for helping my teams achieve successful outcomes. It all started with my positive attitude to take on additional work, even grunt work, and make it succeed. You can do the same.

I've found that those who volunteer in the workplace tend to be the up-and-comers. They're the go-getters, the ones who eventually will be promoted. When I ask for a volunteer to speak on a weekend, they are the first to volunteer. They go above and beyond to succeed and set themselves apart from everyone else in the office. They sacrifice some of their precious free time to do the extra work that many of their peers don't want to do. I see these workers grow as they take on additional challenges. Not only do they become adept at problem-solving and achieving results, they also tend to be my top performers. They stand out, and their "star" rises to the top as a result. When they put in for a promotion, there's no doubt I will remember all of their good deeds and hard work.

Volunteering for extra work and taking on additional challenges provides you ample opportunities to get noticed and get promoted. Yes, it is more work, more time, and more effort for the same pay. But it is an investment in your future with the organization that you cannot afford to miss. While volunteering is a sacrifice in the short term, it will pay off in the long term—and well. When the chance comes your way, get your hand up and volunteer. You are not Billy going to war, you're an employee who will set yourself apart from everyone else—and reap the rewards.

One word of caution if you are going to volunteer, with greater visibility comes greater expectations. A regional or national team can make you or it can hurt you. Make sure you remain committed to the group's success first and foremost. Ensure you are giving it your all and contributing over and above what's asked of you. Make a good impression on your fellow team members and those who will be reviewing team results. Your goal is to get invited to participate in more workgroups in the future. And remember, when the group you are part of succeeds, so will you.

Another strategy that will get you noticed—and that's closely tied to volunteering—is taking the initiative. When you see something that needs to be done, act on it instead of waiting to be told what to do. Take the initiative to tackle and solve a problem and make a difference in your workplace—no matter how big or small the impact may be. When my agency transitioned to electronic files, it left thousands of old paper files sitting in filing cabinets in our office. I could have ignored the files and left them there for someone else to deal with. But that's not me. I took the initiative with my staff to clean out the old files and get as much as possible into the new system. This allowed us to significantly reduce the space needed for filing cabinets and proved a wise decision for the future of remote working. Nobody required me to take this action, but it was the correct thing to do.

Taking the initiative isn't always so easy. In fact, sometimes it can be really complicated. When I was the division administrator in Illinois, the state was under-expending its federal grant funds to improve truck safety on the highway. They actually had money in reserve just waiting to be spent, and yet nothing was being done. My agency wouldn't even take action. Even though they wanted the state to spend the money, year after year they allowed them to underspend. The rollover of funds was excessive and frustrating to see. Those funds were intended to be used for highway safety improvements that could potentially save lives. Instead, they were unused, piling up and people were still dying. I had to act.

I could've sat there and done nothing. But I knew the problem would eventually boil over if left as it was. Something needed to be done. Somehow I needed to get the state to spend more money. Doing so meant going to the top of their chain of command, to the Illinois secretary of transportation. I would have to go around lower-level supervisors of his agency, who could not or would not act. It was a daunting task. The secretary might not like that I was bringing the matter up. And his subordinates might get really upset with me. And my boss was concerned about pushing the state too hard. What if it didn't work? What if it backfired? What if?

*"Leaders don't wait for the go-ahead
before taking action."*

Since taking the initiative is often a little risky, it's always a good idea to weigh the available options. I knew that my agency would eventually tell me to do something about the fact that the state was underspending its federal grant money. But how does that make me look if I wait around to be told to do something that I already know needs to be done? It wasn't going to make me stand out, that was for sure. So I wrote a letter to the Illinois secretary of transportation. In it, I outlined the issue and told him how it was hurting the state. I asked him to take action and increase the use of federal grant funds designed to save lives on Illinois highways. I sent the letter and waited.

Now I didn't have to put myself in the position of potentially stirring up a hornet's nest. I could've waited for my boss to tell me what to do. That way, he would take the blame if it failed miserably, not me. But that isn't what a leader does. A leader takes the initiative, even when risk is involved.

U.S. General George Patton is a perfect example of this. During World War II, he was leading his troops through Belgium to the German border when he received a message from headquarters. Don't bother trying to capture the German city of Trier, it said, since it would take four divisions of troops to do so. But, unknown to his superiors, General Patton had already captured Trier and was on German territory, ready to advance further. Patton's reply to his superiors was classic. "Have taken Trier with two divisions. Do you want me to give it back?"[1] *That's* leadership.

Leaders don't wait for the go-ahead before taking action. When my employees take the initiative in their work, it shows me they care not only about their job but about the agency. As the DA in California, I asked my team of bus inspectors to start increasing the number of safety inspections they did. The challenge was that federal law only allowed buses to be inspected under certain circumstances, such as when they were stopped and not loaded with passengers. My inspectors had to find a solution. So they took the initiative and asked the operators of Indian-owned casinos if they could inspect buses on casino property. Casinos were perfect locations where the passengers left a bus for hours at a time. This left empty buses and their drivers sitting in parking lots. A good place for our folks to inspect. My inspectors set up face-to-face meetings with the management at these casinos to discuss their proposals. In some cases, in addition to management officials, my inspectors were required to meet with tribal elders to obtain approval.

As a result of their efforts, a number of casinos agreed to permit them to inspect buses on their property. My

---

1   https://www.britannica.com/biography/George-Smith-Patton

team later told me that the tribal elders and management officials they met with only approved their request because they trusted our inspectors as individuals. They did not owe the U.S. government anything, but their decision had a huge impact on bus safety. Our folks were able to inspect hundreds more buses each year because of these agreements. And it was all because my employees took the initiative in line with my direction.

**

When the Illinois transportation secretary finally responded to my letter, I was nervous. Would it be good or bad? What was my boss going to say if the secretary was upset because of my actions? All of these thoughts raced through my mind as I opened his response letter. But regardless of the outcome, I knew I did the right thing. I took action when it was needed, and I was fully prepared to defend my actions if need be.

Thankfully, the secretary's response was positive. He acknowledged the problem and said he would put a plan in place to address my concerns. Over time, he kept his word and spent the state's federal grants funds more quickly. Needless to say, I was elated. I couldn't have been more proud of myself for taking the initiative even though it was risky. Everyone was happy—my boss, the agency, my team—and I got noticed in the process. Contrast this with how I would have looked if my boss finally had to get on me to do something about the problem. Even if the results were the same, I would have looked very different to my superiors.

Don't wait for others to tell you to do something that you know needs to be done. When you take the initiative on problems, you get noticed as a leader. Your efforts won't always be successful, and that's okay. I'd rather have my employees take the initiative and fail than constantly wait around for me to tell them what to do. The worst option is to do nothing and stay stuck where you are.

Taking the initiative in the workplace is not like gambling, where you put everything on the table and roll the dice. It's a reasonable, thought-out action designed to solve a problem. It isn't contrary to existing workplace policy or law. If an initiative fails, it won't result in the downfall of the organization. If the tribal elders at the casinos had told my team no, they couldn't inspect buses on casino property, that would not have caused my agency to collapse.

Before taking action, it's wise to ask yourself a few questions about what you want to do. What is the risk and reward of doing this? Do I have the capacity in my position to initiate this? Is this going to get me fired? Is it going to damage my organization in any way if it fails? What happens if it fails? What happens if I do nothing? In my career, I've found that the benefits of taking the initiative are worth far more than the risk of doing nothing. I cannot recall once in my thirty years of government service when my superiors were upset with me for taking the initiative on an issue. On the contrary, I was often thanked, noticed, and given awards for taking measured risks and producing big results.

As you follow these tips for getting noticed in the workplace, above all else, remember to do your job. Nothing speaks more loudly on your behalf and gets you noticed more than doing a great job. And nothing gets you more negative visibility than when you don't do your job. I know it sounds so simple, but people forget this all the time. Your job output is your record, and you should be proud to wear it on your sleeve. When you do fantastic work, you get noticed. When you show up on time, don't cause issues, and get results, you get noticed. Nothing can take the place of doing a good job right where you are at. I've seen so many individuals spend more time trying to politic themselves into a promotion instead of just doing their job as best they can. Don't focus so much on the job that you want that you neglect to do your current job well. Why would someone promote you if you are failing to successfully manage your current responsibilities?

When you put all of your attention, focus, and skill into your current work, it will pay off. Your immediate supervisor will take notice, and guess who they talk to? Other supervisors who may want to promote you! Employees can say all the right words, look the part, and answer every interview question for a promotion, but at the end of the day, it is their work record that speaks volumes.

Strive to be the best where you are right now. It's okay to look forward to the future and dream—in fact, it's encouraged. It's perfectly fine to see yourself being promoted to bigger and better positions. It's great to aspire to reach the top. But don't forget about the here and now. Right now is where you get noticed for the promotions that will take you to where you want to be.

Having a positive outlook, volunteering for extra work, taking the initiative and doing your current job well all help you get noticed in the workplace. Use each of these tools to your advantage and you will become more visible wherever you are. Now go get noticed for the right reasons - and look your best.

Chapter 26
Lessons in Getting Noticed
Key Takeaways and Applied Knowledge

Take it Further: Take a break to visualize how your career might change for the better by applying the chapter's lessons.

Chapter 27

THE MAGIC NUMBER

Lessons in Span of Control

Performance numbers, goal numbers, product numbers, production numbers, quarterly numbers—there are a lot of numbers you need to know and manage as a leader. But there's one number in particular that will control you if you don't control it. It can be your friend or your foe. If it's too high, it can cause negative issues, but if it's too low, it can cause inefficiency. Not many leaders know this number exists, but it is crucial to succeeding in the workplace. You're probably wondering by now what this mysterious number is. It's called the span of control number—sometimes the span of control ratio—and you need to be very careful with it.

The span of control number is used to determine how many employees one person can feasibly supervise. You look at a big corporation with thousands of employees and wonder how one CEO leads and manages all those employees. And the answer is they don't. A CEO can't manage thousands of employees, it's impossible! What these CEOs have is a small team of executives whom they lead, who in turn lead others, and on and on to manage every employee. But what exactly is the number of people that one supervisor can effectively lead and manage?

In the early 1900s, Sir Ian Hamilton, a British General, began studying this question. He came to the remarkable conclusion that three to six was the ideal number of direct reports a leader should have to be the most effective and efficient in their army.[1] Surprisingly, the span of control number is usually lower than you might think. And putting such low numbers of direct reports into practice makes for an incredibly efficient operation.

During my time in the U.S. Marine Corps Reserves, I was in an infantry unit. Our one company had over 300 Marines, and together with our battalion, regiment and division, that number was well into the thousands. Despite our large numbers, most of the leadership and management was concentrated in small platoons of thirty to forty Marines. Within each platoon, there were three squads of twelve Marines and within each squad, there were three fire teams of three to four Marines.

The Marines supervised thousands of men and women through these small groups, each led by a squad or fire team leader. The squad leader in particular, became the main point of leadership for the group. In addition to providing their group directions and job assignments, it was their job to ensure each Marine had chow, water, ammunition, and supplies. And during actual combat, it is these squad leaders who control, direct, and manage the

---

[1]   Sir Ian Hamilton, *The Soul and Body of an Army*, 1921

fight. As a Marine rifleman, I depended on my squad leader more than anyone else in the unit.

> *"Such a structure enables the Marine Corps to lead thousands of Marines at the ground level efficiently. That's span of control, and it works wonderfully in times of combat."*

When Marine infantry units are in combat, they must move quickly since the situation can—and often does—change on a dime. If a company commander, who usually oversees 300 Marines, needs to attack or reposition his forces, he calls in the platoon leaders who report directly to him. He gives them his plans, who then pass along the plans to the squad leaders, who then pass along the plans to the fire team leaders or to the Marines in their group. The company commander certainly doesn't have the time to meet with every single Marine, explain the plan of attack, and take questions. He can't supervise everyone at one time and move them along a battlefield that could stretch out for miles.

The span of control tactic ensures that every Marine has proper leadership at all times and enables lines of communication to flow smoothly from the upper rungs of leadership to every Marine in the company. This system has been tested by the most difficult of circumstances and has stood the test of time.

Numerous studies have been conducted on the ideal span of control number since Sir Ian Hamilton studied the issue in the early 1900s. Varying numbers have been proposed to be the best and most efficient ones for workplaces everywhere. But in the end, the ideal span of control number is the one that works best for you. Whichever one gives you the most control and efficiency in your workplace is the one you need to stick with. But how, precisely, do you determine that? There are some guidelines and some warnings to help you figure out which span of control number is right for you.

The difficulty of the task at hand affects the span of control, as does your proximity to the employees. More complex work lowers the number of employees you can effectively supervise since the difficulty of the work often places more burden on the supervisor. Take investigative work, for example. Reviewing evidence and selecting proper regulatory citations is difficult work and requires more oversight. In addition, the employees performing these jobs often work in remote locations and frequently deal with members of the public. In situations like this, you will have more work to do in supervising these employees, which means your span of control number should be lower so you can handle your responsibilities. On the other hand, if you supervise employees on a production line who are always in front of you and don't interact with external customers, your span of control can be larger since you will likely have the capacity to supervise more people.

A crucial aspect to know about the span of control is that the number of relationships a superior must manage rises exponentially after the fourth subordinate.[2] If you have four employees who directly report to you, and I give you one more, that doesn't seem like a large increase, right? But you aren't supervising just one more employee. You are also overseeing the interactions that additional employee has with their fellow employees, clients, members of the public, and yourself as the supervisor. Adding a fifth subordinate roughly doubles the complexity of relationships, and adding a sixth would double it again. As more direct reports are added to you, your workload increases substantially. Instead of simply *adding* to your workload, more employees actually *multiply* it. It's been calculated that for 12 subordinates, the total number of relationships that might demand a supervisor's attention is an astounding 24,564.[3] Wow!

It's a punishing increase that can quickly take its toll on a leader and a business. Going beyond the span of control number ultimately sets up leaders for failure since they cannot possibly handle all of the responsibilities that come with supervising so many employees. Now you see what an incredibly important number this is!

What is amazing to me is that the number suggested by Sir Ian Hamilton of three to six direct reports is very

---

2 Fred Nichols, *The Span of Control and the Formulas of V.A. Graicunas,* Distance Consulting, 2011, p. 3
3 See footnote 2, p. 4

close to what I've experienced in my line of work. In fact, in the last few years of my career with the government, I had seven employees who reported directly to me. And those seven supervised others, who supervised others, and so on to provide direct supervision to sixty-five employees. I worked with those seven supervisors to indirectly affect the work of all sixty-five. I never sent messages to all sixty-five employees, but only to the seven supervisors. The performance goals I wanted my division to achieve were never communicated to all sixty-five at once but given to the seven, who then took these expectations, goals, and communication to their leads to pass on to their respective units. Eventually, everyone was on the same page.

There was no way I could have successfully managed sixty-five employees at once! However, by having a small group of supervisors to work with daily, I handled my tasks and responsibilities much more efficiently. And as a result, I was able to be a much more effective leader for my organization.

But I also know what it's like to feel overwhelmed by the number of employees to supervise. At one point, I supervised thirteen to fifteen employees, a mix of remote workers, investigators and office staff. It was a difficult time for me. I was prevented from operating at my fullest potential due to being bogged down with employee supervision. And when I was busy putting out fires things became even more challenging. It's not something I would ever want to return to.

Evaluating your duties and those of your employees is crucial to figuring out the correct span of control number for you. It's always going to be lower than you think. The number should enable you to focus on your work, set your goals, and lead so that you feel in control of what's happening in your workplace. You could look at similar businesses in your line of work and evaluate their span of control number to help you figure out what yours should be.

Keep in mind that cost is an issue when determining the span of control. Obviously, it costs more money to employ more supervisors. And since business efficiency is paramount to success, having more supervision than necessary isn't good. But having the wrong span of control ratio will cause more harm and cost more than it saves. Nobody has infinite time to manage employees.

There are some measures you can take to help if you feel that you are supervising too many employees right now. First, learn how to delegate. Delegating work not only removes tasks from your to-do list but also gives your employees opportunities to take on more responsibility. As you delegate, you manage for results which gives you more time to focus on those things that bring success to your organization. Delegation helps you, it helps your employees and it helps mitigate a high span of control number.

Second, empower your employees to make decisions on their own. I allowed my employees to make decisions that I deemed to be safe for them to make. If they messed up, their mistake wasn't going to sink the ship. And by doing so, I was freed from smaller-level tasks to work on higher-level priorities. Let's say when I had thirteen direct reports, they were empowered to make some decisions without my approval. Think for a moment how much time was saved from not having those individuals emailing and calling me on minor issues! Now multiply this time savings over a week or month and you begin to see the benefits empowerment brings to the span of control equation.

And finally, work towards hiring more management if needed to get to the number that works best for your situation. I realize this is not a quick solution as resources and hiring approval are not always easy to obtain. However, I've been in these situations and continued requesting and documenting why such positions were necessary. In time, I received most of the positions I asked for because I was persistent and here's that word again - patient.

Although complex, the span of control number is the magic number you need to succeed. Whether heading into your first leadership position or struggling to manage the number of employees you already have, determining the proper level of control is key. So keep at it, delegate, empower, and work toward that magic number that works for you and your workplace.

Chapter 27
Lessons in Span of Control
Key Takeaways and Applied Knowledge

Take it Further: Consider how the chapter relates to your work situation. How would you rate your current span of control? What positive changes could you initiate in this area?

Chapter 28

WE'RE ALL HUMAN

Lessons in Personal Wellbeing

We've now covered the methods you need to know to be an effective leader in your workplace. I know that with time and patience, you will get positive results from following these methods, just as I have in my career. Before starting your leadership journey, I want to leave you with a few important thoughts. First, you will make mistakes as you endeavor to lead others. It's inevitable. Don't let those mistakes hurt you, though. Instead, learn from them. Let mistakes be an opportunity to grow as a person. For example, I've lost control of my tongue before, but then I learned how to control it better moving forward. Now, I've almost mastered the habit. Don't kick yourself too hard when you make a mistake. We're all human and will make mistakes along the way.

> *"...You will make mistakes as you endeavor to lead others. It's inevitable. Don't let those mistakes hurt you, though. Instead, learn from them. Let mistakes be an opportunity to grow as a person."*

Sometimes your best plans will fall through and fail. Being a leader means continually analyzing what went wrong and determining to try it again in a different way next time. No matter what, don't stop moving forward.

Someone once told me not to get too high when everything is going great and don't get too low when things aren't going your way. Keeping an even mindset in leadership is so crucial. Don't celebrate too much when you win and don't drown too much in sorrow when you lose. I've taken that advice many times throughout my career.

Finally, take care of yourself physically. Being a leader is demanding work. There are so many pressures that come to bear on you daily, weekly, monthly, and yearly. Whether it's pressure for results, timeliness, quality or pressure from those above or issues with those below you, the many responsibilities and demands can—and will—take a toll. If you don't deal with these pressures in a healthy manner, they will hurt you.

Have you ever noticed those big cargo tankers going down the road that carry gasoline? They look like big shiny cans and have placards on them to warn about the flammability of the contents. But just as deadly as the ignition of its contents is the pressure the gas can exert on the inside of the tank. The pressure alone can cause the tank to explode like a bomb detonating. Despite such a huge danger, you rarely if ever see these gas tankers blowing up. Why? Each tank has a pressure relief valve built in to release pressure when it hits a critical point. With just this one little valve, the dangerous pressure in the tank is safely released, saving the tank and everyone around it. It's a simple device but has a huge impact on the safe transportation of gasoline.

Your body similarly needs a Pressure Relief Valve (PRV) to let go of the stress that builds upon you as a leader. Just like the pressure in a cargo tank, stress builds inside of you and can reach a critical point. While stress is natural and a part of every job, it can induce serious physical and mental health problems when it's allowed to build unchecked with no release. It will consume you if it isn't dealt with properly. To be successful as a leader, you must make sure that the stress exerted upon you doesn't reach the level where it becomes unhealthy and damaging. In other words, you too need to have a pressure relief valve.

Now, there is a right way and a wrong way to deal with stress. For starters, your PRV cannot be alcohol, tobacco, or drugs of any kind. Using these to cope with stress is dangerous and will only cause more problems in the long run. The PRVs you and I need are the simple yet powerful things in life that give us joy and take our minds off of work.

Every leader needs to find the activity that works best for them. No matter what it is, the PRV should involve some type of physical activity that serves as an outlet for both mind and body to unwind and release pent-up stress.

"Your body similarly needs a Pressure Relief Valve (PRV) to let go of the stress that builds upon you as a leader. Just like the pressure in a cargo tank, stress builds inside of you and can reach a critical point."

My daily PRV was as simple as taking my dog for an evening walk around our neighborhood. With each step I took I could feel the stress begin to melt away. As we walked, I would recall the stressful moments from the day in my mind, analyze them, and then let them go both mentally and physically. Some nights I started my walk upset about what happened at work that day and ready to explode at anything that crossed my path. But by the time I returned from the walk, I was calm, more relaxed and the pressure from the stress of the day was gone. I quickly realized how much I needed those walks—even more so than my dog!

I soon realized I needed more than just daily walks to unwind from work. I incorporated weekly and monthly activities into my schedule that further helped me release stress and have fun. I biked, hiked, took camping trips, and sometimes spent time off at home building model airplanes or coding, which has always been a favorite pastime of mine. These activities, these little inexpensive valves, saved my health. And in the process, they allowed me to physically and mentally prepare to continue handling my job and its many responsibilities well.

I don't know what your PRV needs to be—but you do. Maybe it's yoga or playing video games. Perhaps it's playing with your children before bedtime or running. You don't have to spend large amounts of time on these activities for them to be effective. Find what gives you a good night's rest. Find what lowers your blood pressure and makes you feel good. Find an activity you enjoy. And once you find it, make it a daily, weekly, and monthly habit. Your health depends on it. You'll find yourself more relaxed and at peace when you're at home. And you'll be renewed to tackle tomorrow's challenges like the strong, effective leader you are.

And with that, you have everything you need to be a successful leader. Now it's time for you to step up and become the leader you were made to be. You can do it!

I wish you all the best.

Steve Mattioli

Chapter 28
Lessons in Personal Wellbeing
Key Takeaways and Applied Knowledge

Take it Further: Share this book with a friend or colleague who might benefit from it.

Acknowledgments

This book was the result of thirty years of leadership experience working with people from different backgrounds and organizations. While too numerous to name, I want to thank everyone I worked with over those years. I had the opportunity to engage with some of the best leaders and people throughout my career. Each person, in some way, helped me develop my skills, find those inner flaws, and helped me be a better person. I served with some of the finest, who inspired me with their dedication and hard work. I'll always be grateful to each one of you.

I could not have written this book without the support and love of my family. They encouraged me throughout the process and helped me when I needed it most. Special thanks to my wife Dottie and daughter Rachel who spent hours proofreading my drafts and helping me smooth out my thoughts and words.

Finally, I want to thank God for his provision and blessing in my life. I was given the privilege to lead others and never took it for granted. Looking back in hindsight, God wrote my story so that I could share it and help others. God allowed me to see the good in people and how important it was to lead in a manner that reflected his goodness and grace. God helped me through difficult situations, and I relied on his word and prayer throughout my career. I wanted my leadership to reflect Jesus, my Lord and Savior. All the success I enjoyed I owe to him, who was always by my side guiding me every step of the way.

Connect with the Author

I enjoyed writing this book and sharing my insights into leadership with you. I plan to continue teaching and helping others succeed as leaders.

Please visit my website at MattioliSolutions.com for more leadership articles, training videos, and other helpful resources for leaders. And please sign up for our email list to receive a free offer when you visit my site.

I also enjoy hearing from you, whether you have questions, comments, or need additional information on leadership training. Please contact me at: Steve.Mattioli@icloud.com.